BARRON'S BOOK NOTES

CHARLES DICKENS'S

Oliver Twist

BARRON'S BOOK NOTES

CHARLES DICKENS'S

Oliver Twist

BY

Virginia B. Morris
Associate Professor of English
John Jay College, City University of New York

SERIES COORDINATOR
Murray Bromberg
Principal, Wang High School of Queens
Holliswood, New York

Past President
High School Principals Association of New York City

BARRON'S EDUCATIONAL SERIES, INC.

ACKNOWLEDGMENTS

Our thanks to Milton Katz and Julius Liebb for their advisory assistance on the *Book Notes* series. Thanks also to Holly Hughes, who made a substantial editorial contribution to this book.

All inquiries should be addressed to:
Barron's Educational Series, Inc.
113 Crossways Park Drive
Woodbury, New York 11797

Library of Congress Catalog Card No. 85-4068

International Standard Book No. 0-8120-3532-1

Library of Congress Cataloging in Publication Data
Morris, Virginia B.
    Charles Dickens's Oliver Twist.

    (Barron's book notes)
    Bibliography: p. 95
    Summary: A guide to reading "Oliver Twist" with a critical and appreciative mind encouraging analysis of plot, style, form, and structure. Also includes background on the author's life and times, sample tests, term paper suggestions, and a reading list.
    1. Dickens, Charles, 1812–1870. Oliver Twist.
[1. Dickens, Charles, 1812–1870. Oliver Twist.
2. English literature—History and criticism] I. Title.
II. Series.
PR4567.M6   1985   823'.8   85-4068

    ISBN 0-7641-9161-6

PRINTED IN THE UNITED STATES OF AMERICA

34   550   98765432

CONTENTS

ADVISORY BOARD

We wish to thank the following educators who helped us focus our *Book Notes* series to meet student needs and critiqued our manuscripts to provide quality materials.

Sandra Dunn, English Teacher
Hempstead High School, Hempstead, New York

Lawrence J. Epstein, Associate Professor of English
Suffolk County Community College, Selden, New York

Leonard Gardner, Lecturer, English Department
State University of New York at Stony Brook

Beverly A. Haley, Member, Advisory Committee
National Council of Teachers of English Student
Guide Series, Fort Morgan, Colorado

Elaine C. Johnson, English Teacher
Tamalpais Union High School District
Mill Valley, California

Marvin J. LaHood, Professor of English
State University of New York College at Buffalo

Robert Lecker, Associate Professor of English
McGill University, Montréal, Québec, Canada

David E. Manly, Professor of Educational Studies
State University of New York College at Geneseo

Bruce Miller, Associate Professor of Education
State University of New York at Buffalo

Frank O'Hare, Professor of English and
Director of Writing
Ohio State University, Columbus, Ohio

Faith Z. Schullstrom, Member, Executive Committee
National Council of Teachers of English
Director of Curriculum and Instruction
Guilderland Central School District, New York

Mattie C. Williams, Director, Bureau of Language Arts
Chicago Public Schools, Chicago, Illinois

HOW TO USE THIS BOOK

You have to know how to approach literature in order to get the most out of it. This *Barron's Book Notes* volume follows a plan based on methods used by some of the best students to read a work of literature.

Begin with the guide's section on the author's life and times. As you read, try to form a clear picture of the author's personality, circumstances, and motives for writing the work. This background usually will make it easier for you to hear the author's tone of voice, and follow where the author is heading.

Then go over the rest of the introductory material—such sections as those on the plot, characters, setting, themes, and style of the work. Underline, or write down in your notebook, particular things to watch for, such as contrasts between characters and repeated literary devices. At this point, you may want to develop a system of symbols to use in marking your text as you read. (Of course, you should only mark up a book you own, not one that belongs to another person or a school.) Perhaps you will want to use a different letter for each character's name, a different number for each major theme of the book, a different color for each important symbol or literary device. Be prepared to mark up the pages of your book as you read. Put your marks in the margins so you can find them again easily.

Now comes the moment you've been waiting for—the time to start reading the work of literature. You may want to put aside your *Barron's Book Notes* volume until you've read the work all the way through. Or you may want to alternate, reading the *Book Notes* analysis of each section as soon as you have finished reading the corresponding part of the original. Before you move on, reread crucial passages you don't fully understand. (Don't take this guide's analysis for granted—make up your own mind as to what the work means.)

Once you've finished the whole work of literature, you may want to review it right away, so you can firm up your ideas about what it means. You may want to leaf through the book concentrating on passages you marked in reference to one character or one theme. This is also a good time to reread the *Book Notes* introductory material, which pulls together insights on specific topics.

When it comes time to prepare for a test or to write a paper, you'll already have formed ideas about the work. You'll be able to go back through it, refreshing your memory as to the author's exact words and perspective, so that you can support your opinions with evidence drawn straight from the work. Patterns will emerge, and ideas will fall into place; your essay question or term paper will almost write itself. Give yourself a dry run with one of the sample tests in the guide. These tests present both multiple-choice and essay questions. An accompanying section gives answers to the multiple-choice questions as well as suggestions for writing the essays. If you have to select a term paper topic, you may choose one from the list of suggestions in this book. This guide also provides you with a reading list, to help you when you start research for a term paper, and a selection of provocative comments by critics, to spark your thinking before you write.

THE AUTHOR
AND HIS TIMES

Few writers are lucky enough to have their first novels become runaway bestsellers. Yet that is exactly what happened when 25-year-old Charles Dickens published *Oliver Twist* in 1837.

Many readers already knew of young Dickens. As a journalist, he had written, under the pen name Boz, gripping newspaper accounts exposing social conditions in England. In another vein entirely, he had written a bestselling collection of humorous stories called *The Pickwick Papers*. His journalistic sketches showed descriptive power and the ability to influence people's political ideas; *The Pickwick Papers* showed how he could create marvelous characters and sustain lively comic scenes. But with *Oliver Twist*, Dickens surprised everyone by revealing yet another talent—for spinning a rich, suspenseful web of plot.

One reason why *Oliver Twist* was so popular was that Dickens understood what his audience wanted to read and was willing to write it. He gave them sentimental love scenes, a horrifying glimpse of the criminal underworld, a virtuous hero in Oliver, and nasty villains in Bill Sikes and Fagin. And he wrapped it all up in a complicated, puzzling mystery story. Because *Oliver Twist* was published in monthly installments, Dickens could leave his readers in agonizing suspense from month to month. All across England, readers eagerly discussed what had happened in the most recent installment and argued over what they thought would happen in the next one. *Oliver Twist* was a part of everyday conversation, just as top-rated television shows are for us today.

Yet, even though he was young and hungry for fame, Dickens wanted to do more than just entertain. He challenged his readers to consider things they would rather have ignored. He drew for them a picture of London's slums that was shocking in its realism. Victorian authors were not supposed to acknowledge the existence of drunkards and prostitutes, but Dickens did. They were not supposed to use street language, even in dialogue, but Dickens did.

Dickens wasn't the only one concerned about the poor, for poverty and vagrancy had plagued England since the sixteenth century. In 1834, a few years before the publication of *Oliver Twist*, Parliament had passed a Poor Law intended to end some of the worst abuses against the indigent. Yet the provision of the bill didn't go far in providing relief for those who were suffering.

Dickens wanted to do something about the shameful poverty in England. Although his readers didn't know this, poverty had personally scarred Dickens. His family had been quite comfortable when he was born in Portsmouth in 1812, but his parents weren't very skilled at managing money. When he was about 12 years old, his family was confined to debtors' prison, in London, an experience he later wrote about in *Little Dorrit*. Only the money left by his grandmother when she died bailed them out. His knowledge of prison gave Dickens a lifelong obsession with prisoners and inhumane institutions. The hunger and loneliness that tortures Oliver Twist while he is a ward of the parish were very real to Dickens during his own family crisis.

For young Dickens, the lowest point of his life occurred while his family was in prison. For six dreadful months, he was forced to work as an apprentice in a bootblacking factory, pasting labels on bottles of shoe polish. Not only was the work exhausting, the experience was humiliating. In *Oliver Twist* he included a brief episode condemning the apprenticeship system, but it was not until later, in *David Copperfield*, that he could face writing about the factory in detail.

While *Oliver Twist* is not as autobiographical as *David Copperfield*, many other incidents in the novel reflect Dickens' experiences. He deeply regretted not having had more schooling and suggests that in Oliver's eagerness to learn.

In May 1837, his beloved 17 year-old sister-in-law, Mary Hogarth, died, and many readers of *Oliver Twist* think he based the characters of Rose and Nancy on Mary, as a way of working out his intense grief. While Rose survives a dangerous illness, Nancy dies a brutal death. Dickens himself felt Mary had deserted him; similarly, Oliver is terrified that Rose will die and leave him. Dickens was haunted by dreams about Mary, just as Sikes is haunted by a vision of Nancy's eyes after he has killed her.

The criminal underworld of Fagin, Nancy, and Sikes in *Oliver Twist* was as well-known to Dickens as the workhouses and debtors' prisons. As a court reporter and journalist, he had seen the seamy side of urban life. He had met hardened criminals like Sikes and women like Nancy. He had little sympathy for criminals like Fagin, who abuse and cor-

rupt others, yet he knew that there were others—
like Nancy and Charley Bates—who were criminals only because of their environment, and who
might still be reformed. Later he became actively
involved with Urania Cottage, a refuge for home-
less women, including prostitutes. Knowing they
had led rough lives, Urania Cottage was set up as
an environment where they could feel at home and
prepare themselves for a better life. Dickens' sympathy for Nancy is clear in *Oliver Twist*. Typically,
he was motivated to get involved, to try to change
conditions for girls like her before it was too late.

The 1830s were a time of growing concern about
social issues and energetic reform. As a popular
writer and public personality, Dickens had a power
to do good. He could reach a vast middle-class
audience, shocking them into action by his dramatic storytelling. *Oliver Twist*, which began to appear in serial form in 1837, was only the first of
Dickens' novels to increase social concern and help
bring about reform.

Ironically, Dickens' own death at age 58 is linked
inadvertently to *Oliver Twist*. Dickens was a frustrated actor who eagerly took part in amateur and
professional theatrical performances. Reading from
his own works, he drew huge, enthusiastic crowds
whose admission tickets helped to pay the novelist's bills and support his large family. His final
dramatic program, a reading of Nancy's murder
and Sikes' hanging, was physically and emotionally exhausting. His body wasn't equal to the de-
mands he made on it. On June 8, 1870, as he was
working on his final novel, *The Mystery of Edwin
Drood*, he collapsed and died.

THE NOVEL

The Plot

Oliver Twist is born an orphan when his pretty vagrant mother dies in a parish workhouse—to the annoyance of Bumble the beadle. Oliver is raised by parish charity, unloved, underfed, and over-worked. At the age of nine, after he dares to ask for seconds at dinner one night, he is sold as an apprentice to a local undertaker, Mr. Sowerberry. Taunted by another apprentice, Noah Claypole, about his unmarried dead mother, Oliver valiantly gets into a fistfight and is eventually locked in the cellar for punishment. Then, taking matters into his own hands, Oliver runs away to London.

The first person he meets in London is the enthusiastic Artful Dodger, who offers him a home with a "gentleman" named Fagin and his group of boys. Oliver is happy there, until he discovers to his horror that they're thieves. One day, while being trained by other boys, Oliver is falsely arrested for picking an elderly gentleman's pocket. In the courtroom, however, Oliver collapses. He attracts the pity of his accuser, Mr. Brownlow, who takes him home. Oliver gets his first taste of kindness and wealth there as he is nursed back to health.

The first time Oliver leaves the house, Fagin's gang kidnaps him so he won't give evidence against them. Back in the London slums, Oliver earns the affections of a young prostitute named Nancy who sticks up for Oliver when Fagin and her lover, Bill Sikes, try to abuse him.

Unfortunately for Oliver, he's just the right size

to help Sikes commit a robbery, and he is taken along on a dangerous job. But, Oliver is wounded in the attempt and is taken in by the Maylies, the people Sikes wanted to rob.

In the idyllic months that follow, Oliver stays with Mrs. Maylie and her niece Rose and grows to love them. He's sad that their attempts to find Mr. Brownlow are unsuccessful, but otherwise things seem perfect. Rose falls seriously ill but recovers. Rose has other troubles, however; her romance with Henry Maylie is impeded by the fact that, because she thinks she is illegitimate, she's unwilling to damage his political career by marrying him.

Safe as he feels, Oliver dreams one night of his troubled past. When he wakes, the evil Fagin and an unknown companion are lurking outside the window.

One of Fagin's cohorts, a grim fellow named Monks, visits the Bumbles to buy the evidence of Oliver's parentage—a locket left by his mother. Monks throws the locket into a river, then presses Fagin to recapture Oliver and make a thief of him.

Even though Oliver has been away, Nancy often thinks about him. When she overhears conversations between Fagin and his strange accomplice, Monks, she becomes worried that Oliver is in danger. She drugs Sikes and seeks out Rose Maylie who happens to be passing through London. Nancy reveals that Monks is Oliver's half brother, and that, in order to keep an inheritance for himself, Monks may cause harm to Oliver.

Rose finally finds Mr. Brownlow and enlists his help. They meet Nancy on London Bridge to learn more about Monks. When they offer Nancy refuge, she refuses, insisting that she must go home to Sikes, whom she loves even though he is brutal to her. What she doesn't know is that suspicious Fagin has had her followed and that her conversation has been overheard. Angered by Nancy's betrayal, Fagin incites Sikes to such fury that he beats Nancy to death. Brownlow, using Nancy's information, locates Monks. Evil Monks is, ironically, the son of Brownlow's best friend, and Oliver Twist is his illegitimate younger brother. Their father, who hated Monks' mother and loved Oliver's, wrote a will leaving most of his money to the younger son, Oliver—unless he turned out to be a criminal. That is why Monks plotted with Fagin to make Oliver a thief. After wandering around for two days, Sikes is finally tracked down and surrounded by police in a hideout. He hangs himself accidentally while trying to escape. The threat to Oliver is eliminated.

Brownlow forces Monks to reveal the rest of his information: not only is Oliver entitled to a fortune, but his mother was Rose Maylie's sister! All at once, Oliver has money and a family too. The questions about Rose's parents are answered, and she can marry Henry Maylie. Fagin is arrested, convicted, and hanged. His gang is scattered. Monks goes off to America, where he later dies in prison. Mr. Brownlow adopts Oliver and they all live happily in the country.

The Characters
MAJOR CHARACTERS
Oliver Twist
The orphan Oliver is a loving, innocent child. In his rags-to-riches career he finally finds happiness with his aunt, Rose Maylie, and his mentor, Mr. Brownlow. But at birth, his prospects aren't very

bright. His mother dies, leaving him in a public workhouse deprived of affection, education, and adequate food.

Most readers agree that Oliver is generally quiet and shy rather than aggressive. But when he is nine years old, he does two bold things that change his life. At the workhouse, he asks for more food (Chapter II) and when he's an apprentice he beats up Noah Claypole and runs away (Chapters VI and VII). After that, most of the things that happen to him are out of his control. They are the result of luck—either good or bad—or the active intervention of someone else.

When he arrives in London, he finds himself in the clutches of Fagin and his gang of thieves. Twice he is rescued by the very people that Fagin's gang is trying to rob, first Mr. Brownlow, and later Mrs. Maylie. Both times Oliver is ill and must be nursed back to health. Then his half-brother plots to destroy him. Oliver's affectionate nature, along with his weakness and innocence, earn him the pity and love of the good people he meets. At the same time, his goodness makes him the victim of Fagin, Sikes, and Monks because they persistently scheme to turn him into a thief like themselves. Because Oliver discovers that good people are successful and evil ones are punished, he turns out to be a happy, secure, honest person.

Dickens choice of Oliver's name is very revealing, because the boy's story is full of "twists" and turns. These twists are eventually unraveled, and the truth about his family is discovered. The web of crime that he gets entangled in when he lives with Fagin's gang is straightened out—"untwisted"—by the truth Brownlow uncovers.

Some readers feel that Oliver receives less attention as the novel develops than he does in the beginning. These readers suggest that Oliver's personality doesn't change much, and they point out that he's always honest, trusting, and affectionate despite the conditions he lives in. For these readers, the adventures of Nancy, Sikes, and Fagin overshadow Oliver's story even though he is the novel's hero.

To some other readers, Oliver is a powerful character because he symbolizes all abandoned and mistreated children who can be rescued by love. They point out that Dickens uses his skills at creating character to make Oliver particularly appealing. While the subject of an orphan rescued by a generous benefactor was extremely popular in English fiction, Dickens' Oliver Twist is the one best remembered.

Everyone agrees that Oliver's moment of greatest glory comes when he announces to the master of the workhouse: "Please, sir, I want some more."

Mr. Bumble

A beadle's job was to maintain order in churches and other parish institutions, and Mr. Bumble relishes his work—especially keeping the poor in line. He takes a special responsibility for Oliver Twist, from the day he names the infant to the time when people like kindly Brownlow and evil Monks ask for information about the orphan's past. But the evidence that Dickens provides (in Chapters XVII, XXXVII, and XXXVIII) suggests that Bumble's interest is self-serving.

Some readers find Bumble revolting and others find him laughable. His hypocrisy is obvious—he is fat while his clients are thin, and self-important although he expects them to be humble. He revels in his fancy beadle's uniform and pompously wields his cane against whomever is handy. Readers who find him hateful claim he'd sell anybody or anything to make a profit. Those who think he is a harmless buffoon are amused by his grammatical errors, mispronunciations, and "bumbling" incompetence.

Halfway through the book, Bumble changes. When he marries Mrs. Corney he loses his authority. She makes all the decisions, including the one to sell Monks the evidence that proves that Oliver is Monks' brother. After the conspiracy is exposed, Bumble and Mrs. Corney are punished by being removed from their jobs and end up paupers in their own workhouse. Is this a fitting end? Do they deserve it? It all depends on how you read the tone of Dickens' satire on Bumble the beadle.

The Artful Dodger
A talented pickpocket, recruiter, cheater, and wit, Jack Dawkins—known as the Artful Dodger—is a charming rogue. It's no wonder Oliver is impressed by him and follows him willingly to Fagin's school for thieves.

Some readers feel that the Dodger's charms simply make him a bad example for Oliver and the other boys. On the other hand, you might think of him as a misguided, but generous, teenager with the potential to straighten out and be successful.

Consider the way Dickens makes the Dodger more appealing by describing his outrageous clothes and uninhibited manners. At times, he seems more like a free spirit than a conscious crook. Notice that he's arrested before Nancy's murder. Some readers feel Dickens did this so that the Dodger is not implicated in that grim act.

His fans agree that his finest hour is during his trial when he indicts the legal system's treatment of the poor. The court thinks it is sitting in judgment on him. Isn't just the opposite true?

Fagin

Fagin is a master criminal whose specialty is fencing (selling stolen property). He employs a gang of thieves—some of them ignorant children—and is always looking for new recruits. That's why he is glad when the Dodger brings Oliver home. He finds out later from Monks that he can make a profit from turning Oliver into a criminal, and he's even more pleased.

Dickens describes in detail Fagin's unwashed body, his matted red hair, filthy clothing, broken teeth, and black fingernails. His actions aren't very pleasant either. When he meets stronger men, he fawns over them. Most readers find that behavior repulsive and cowardly, as they do his habit of calling people "my dear." They also agree that when Fagin plots against the weak he is ruthless and greedy.

To other readers Fagin seems like a villain straight out of melodrama—skulking through the dark London alleys and called "the old gentleman" (a common nickname for Satan). Even his red hair links him to descriptions of Judas, the betrayer of Jesus. To Victorian readers, the fact that he's a Jew would have indicated that he was greedy, alienated, and unsympathetic. To modern readers, however, Fagin's Jewishness may mean something else—that he's been a victim of prejudice.

Readers who feel some sympathy for Fagin argue that he's just making a living the best way he can. Others say that he behaves as he does because he's been discriminated against, or because the slum environment bred him to crime. They make the point that Dickens' own feelings were mixed—he named Fagin after a boy who had befriended him years earlier, but who was associated with Dickens' most unhappy memories.

Fagin is a man of considerable intelligence, though corrupted by his self-interest. He feels a fleeting moment of pity for Oliver before he sends him off to be Sikes' accomplice. His conscience bothers him after he is condemned to hang. He does have a wry sense of humor and an uncanny ability to understand people. Measure these traits against the evil he does. Is he a villain or a tragic figure?

Mr. Brownlow

Brownlow is a generous man, concerned for other people. Not only does he withdraw his accusation of Oliver, he takes the boy home with him and nurses him out of his fever. True, he is intrigued by the boy's resemblance to a long-forgotten face—Agnes Fleming—but he also develops a fatherly love for the boy.

Brownlow is quick to feel pity for Oliver, yet when he believes he is right he does not hesitate to enforce his will. He insists that Monks must restore the identity and fortune he has stolen from Oliver. He posts a reward for Sikes' capture and is untroubled by Fagin's hanging.

Many readers argue that Brownlow seems to be a caricature of a virtuous man. They point to his attitude toward Nancy, especially his conviction that she should change her lifestyle. Other readers ask: If Brownlow is so virtuous, why does he ignore the law in order to see that his own version of justice triumphs? Though he does more good than harm, to get at Monks he keeps what he knows about Fagin temporarily from the police. Then, to force Monks to reveal his information, he protects him from arrest.

Bill Sikes (Sykes)

Sikes is a bully, a robber, and a murderer. Because he is an ally of Fagin, they are often described as the two faces of evil in the novel: Fagin plans the crimes; Sikes carries them out. The scenes in which Sikes brutally beats Nancy to death and then accidentally hangs himself in his frenzy to escape her haunting eyes are, for many readers, the most frightening moments in the novel. Dickens often selected these passages for his popular dramatic readings.

It's possible that Sikes' evil is so frightening because it is so physical. From the beginning, he is compared to a beast. He uses brute violence to bully, intimidate, and injure other people like Nancy, his unwilling accomplice Oliver, and even clever but cowardly Fagin. Also, Sikes seems to lack much power to reason: He can't figure out Nancy's behavior, and he doesn't realize Fagin is manipulating him.

Some readers explain Sikes' behavior as a result of the brutalizing conditions of the slums in which he lives or his weakness for drinking. Compare him, as a villain, to Fagin. Who seems more evil to you?

Monks (also known as Edward Leeford)

Though Monks first appears late in *Oliver Twist* he is crucial to the novel's outcome, for he is Oliver's half-brother. Because he wants to destroy the boy's chance of inheriting their father's estate, he enlists Fagin to turn Oliver into a criminal. Like Fagin,

Monks is a stock villain, lurking in shadows and uttering curses with a sneer. What lies behind Monks' evil? Since he was born a gentleman and has inherited a fortune, you can't blame poverty or the slums for making him a criminal. Like Fagin, Sikes, and Nancy, Monks lacks family love and moral upbringing. Do you think this accounts for his behavior?

Monks is driven by hatred for his illegitimate half-brother. He goes to great lengths—enlisting Fagin and the Bumbles to insure that Oliver can never gain his inheritance. But his hatred makes him outsmart himself: if he hadn't gone looking for Oliver, he would have kept the entire fortune for himself. He was the only person who knew the boy's identity. Is he destroyed by a jealous passion, or is he a twisted soul who'll use any excuse to commit crimes?

Nancy

Nancy is the hapless product of the slums, the pupil of Fagin, and the abused mistress of Sikes. Although she is a prostitute and an accomplice of crooks, she has the instincts of a good person. She protects Oliver as soon as she sees the threat to him, even though it means landing in trouble with Fagin and Sikes. More perplexingly, she is faithful to Sikes because she loves him, in spite of his abuse.

For many readers, Nancy is the most important character in the novel. They argue that the most memorable scenes are the ones she is in—when she visits Fagin's den, when she waits for Bill to come home, or when she meets with Rose Maylie and Brownlow to help save Oliver.

In contrast, other readers insist that she is just a cliché—the typical prostitute with a heart of gold.

They think that Dickens glosses over the truth about a life like Nancy's. Why do you think Dickens works to make her appealing? Does this make her more or less realistic?

Rose Maylie

At least on the surface, Rose is very different from Nancy. Though both were orphans, Rose was rescued as a child by Mrs. Maylie and grew up secure and protected. Like Nancy, she is compassionate and devoted to Oliver, but in contrast Rose is innocent of the hardships and evils of the world. Idealistically, she refuses to hurt Henry's career by marrying him. Similarly, Nancy risks death to stick with her man. Rose is intelligent enough to recognize that the threat to Oliver is real and wise enough to go to Brownlow for help. She's also open minded enough not to judge Nancy too harshly.

Oliver loves Rose because she is so beautiful and good. She represents, for him, the idea of what a perfect woman should be. After he is "adopted" by Rose and Mrs. Maylie he is able to feel secure and happy.

Because Rose knew what it was like to be rescued from an unhappy childhood, she urgently wants to rescue Oliver, and Nancy too. In that way, she is a representation of all the good instincts of Victorian society.

What upsets Rose the most is the dread that she is illegitimate and therefore stained by the sin of her unknown mother. Later, when she finds out she is Agnes Fleming's sister and Oliver's aunt, she thinks she is tainted by her sister's sin. In these ways, Rose illustrates the great importance her society attached to purity and innocence. Dickens makes clear that she is a pure flower of womanhood.

MINOR CHARACTERS

Sally Thingummy

Sally Thingummy, a pauper, nurses Oliver's mother and steals the locket and ring that holds the key to the orphan's identity.

Agnes Fleming

Agnes Fleming is Oliver's mother. She left home in shame and died when her illegitimate child was born.

Mr. Sowerberry

An undertaker, Mr. Sowerberry accepts Oliver as an apprentice mourner. He is forced by his wife's cruelty to abuse the boy until Oliver runs away.

Noah Claypole

A charity boy, Noah Claypole torments Oliver. He is employed by Fagin, under the alias of Bolter, and spies on Nancy. He ends up as a police informer.

Charley Bates

Charley Bates belongs to Fagin's gang. He is so disgusted by Sikes' evil ways that he gives up crime and becomes a farmer.

Bet (Betsy)

Bet is a whore like Nancy. She loses her sanity when she is required to identify Nancy's corpse.

Fang

Fang is a police magistrate and represents the worst abuses of judicial power. Dickens modeled him on a real-life magistrate named Laing who was removed from office in 1838.

Mrs. Bedwin

Mrs. Bedwin, Brownlow's housekeeper, cares for Oliver and provides his first real mothering when Brownlow rescues him from Fang.

Mr. Grimwig

Mr. Grimwig is Brownlow's friend. He has a tender heart under his gruff exterior and joins the effort to secure Oliver's inheritance after initially doubting the boy.

Toby Crackit

Toby Crackit is a housebreaker who works with Sikes.

Mrs. Corney (later Mrs. Bumble)

She runs the workhouse where Oliver was born. A greedy person, she retrieves Agnes Fleming's treasures from Old Sally and sells them to Monks.

Dr. Losberne

Dr. Losberne, the Maylie's physician, treats Oliver for his wound and conspires with the Maylies to protect Oliver from the police and give him a chance in life. He is part of the group that insures Oliver's future. Sometimes his enthusiasm gets him into trouble.

Henry (Harry) Maylie

Henry Maylie loves Rose and wants to marry her, but she refuses because she believes she is illegitimate and therefore might hurt his chances to win elections. To win Rose, Henry gives up a political career and becomes a clergyman.

Other Elements
SETTING

The major action of *Oliver Twist* moves back and forth between two worlds: the filthy slums of London and the clean, comfortable houses of Brownlow and the Maylies. The first world is real and frightening, while the latter is idealized, almost dreamlike, in its safety and beauty.

The world of London is a world of crime. Things happen there at night, in dark alleys and in abandoned, unlighted buildings. You can find examples in Chapter XV, when Oliver is kidnapped, and in Chapter XXVI, when Fagin meets Monks. Such darkness suggests that evil dominates this world. The rain and fog enveloping the city seem to intensify the dismal atmosphere. You'll notice that Dickens often uses weather conditions to aid in setting a scene. In *Oliver Twist* bad things often happen in bad weather.

In contrast to Fagin's London, the sunlit days and fragrant flowers of the Maylies' cottage (in Chapters XXXIV and XXXV) or the handsome library at Brownlow's (in Chapters XIV and XLI) teem with goodness and health. Many readers feel that the scenes set in these places are less memorable than those in the slums.

The setting changes frequently, in no predictable pattern, but the greatest number of scenes are set in London. The following table shows the movement in the novel from setting to setting.

Oliver's Birthplace	London Slums	Brownlow's House	Maylies' Home or Cottage
Chapters 1–7	Chapters 8–11,13	Chapters 12,14	Chapters 22
part of 17	15,16	part of 17	28–36
23–24	18–21,25	41,49	
27,37	26,38,39		
	42–48,50,52		

Chapter 40 takes place in a London hotel and Chapter 53 at an unnamed country village.

THEMES

There is not much difference of opinion about what Dickens intended *Oliver Twist* to communicate to readers. The following are major themes of the novel.

1. THE INFLUENCE OF THE ENVIRONMENT

Do living conditions determine what happens to people? If so, we are to believe that those of Dickens' people who are deprived of good influences are doomed, while those who enjoy love and security flourish. Oliver, for example, is rescued in time, while Nancy cannot escape death. Dickens depicts the degrading effects of poverty, especially hunger, which turns humans into struggling animals. Dickens may also be arguing that criminals are made, not born. Do you think Dickens is right? Does the influence of environment explain the bad things done by people?

2. ALIENATION

People who are emotionally or physically deprived become cut off from human interaction. Sometimes this alienation from other people makes them withdrawn and passive, like Oliver, who is terrified of being abandoned. Consider also Sikes' aggression, Nancy's depression, or Monks' vindictiveness, as results of alienation. Is Dickens saying that, whatever its cause or effect, alienation is destructive?

3. THE POWER OF TRUE LOVE

Many forms of love appear in *Oliver Twist*, whether between man and woman or parent and child (including adopted children). Dickens seems to suggest that affection is the only source of real

strength. Brownlow's love saves Oliver. Rose and
Henry find happiness together after all their suf-
fering. But love is not successful if it is one-sided.
Nancy's love for Bill, though sincere on her part,
fails because it is not returned. Love also fails when
it is motivated by greed or self-advantage: The
Bumbles' marriage and the relationship between
Noah and Charlotte mock true love.

4.   CHARITY

Oliver Twist suggests that charity, like love, must
be honest to have integrity. Dickens indicates that
true concern for people is found in individuals, not
in institutions. The charity that succeeds in *Oliver
Twist* is the generosity of Brownlow and Mrs. Maylie. The workhouse fails. As you read, you'll want
to think about the accuracy of Dickens' viewpoint.

5.   THE PROCESS OF GROWING UP

Oliver Twist is about growing up. Many of the
characters are young, and they must make choices
about their future. Oliver, the novel's main character, is the most obvious example. Nancy, Rose,
Harry, the Dodger, and Charley make choices too,
and must live with the consequences. Why do you
think that—with the possible exception of the
Dodger—all of their instincts are right? What does
that tell you about Dickens' attitude at this point
in his life? Do you agree with him?

6.   THE POWER OF MORALITY

Mrs. Maylie and Mr. Brownlow don't shun Oliver
or Rose because they're illegitimate or condemn
Nancy for her sexual behavior. Yet Dickens leaves
no doubt that Nancy must pay the price of sin—
death—as Oliver's mother Agnes had. In this way,
Oliver Twist conforms to Victorian morality. Our

modern attitudes toward sexuality are different. Do you think the novel still has relevance for readers, or is it too old-fashioned and narrow-minded?

POINT OF VIEW

A third person, omniscient narrator—a narrator who isn't a character but who knows everything that is happening and what all of the characters are thinking and doing—tells the story most of the time in *Oliver Twist*. The narrator describes events and repeats conversations so that you can understand and evaluate what is going on. The court scene in Chapter XI illustrates how an omniscient narrator tells a story, and so does Chapter L when Sikes is cornered. Most readers agree that Dickens' narrator is fairly objective and reports things accurately. But sometimes the narrator gives details that emphasize a character's bad qualities. Then he is trying to influence your reaction to the character. Look at the descriptions of Gamfield, Sikes, and Fagin, for examples.

Occasionally the narrator interrupts the story he is telling, and speaking in his own voice, as "I", urges you to accept particular ideas. Near the end of Chapter XII, for example, the narrator explains why Charley and the Dodger helped chase Oliver and called him a thief. The narrator's personal involvement emphasizes his concern for making his satiric points.

When a writer changes from one narrator to another, it is usually to draw attention to the subject being discussed. Some readers believe that the first-person narrator sections of *Oliver Twist* resemble the journalistic sketches Dickens was accustomed to writing. The shifts may signal the crusading purpose that was as important to Dickens as telling an exciting story.

STYLE

Oliver Twist is written in many different styles. At times the dialogue is lean and dramatic as, for instance, during Nancy's murder. The story develops quickly and there are very few descriptive details that aren't directly related to the murder. Similarly, when Dickens' wit is at its sharpest, the language slashes at phoniness and hypocrisy (for example, in Chapter XXXVII). His comic exaggerations, in descriptions of Bumble or the Bow Street Runners for instance, make most readers chuckle.

Elsewhere, though, the language may seem stilted and artificial to you because of the long, winding sentences full of colons, semicolons, and parentheses. Dickens' language can also be very sentimental. (Look at the love scenes between Rose and Henry or the description of Oliver at the beginning of Chapter XXX.)

Remember that this was Dickens' first novel and he was still learning the technique of writing a long book. But his work as a reporter had trained him to use detail in the scenes that describe the slums. His years of theater-going had prepared him to build scenes of suspense.

Though Dickens was trying to describe the world realistically, the language doesn't always show how people in the slums talked. Not even Sikes uses four-letter words. Explicit sexual scenes are left out too. Dickens wanted his book to appeal to as wide an audience as possible, and he didn't want to offend his readers. On the other hand, Dickens makes use of some street slang, especially the slang of thieves, which adds a distinct flavor to the story. For example, look at the way the Artful Dodger talks.

The language in *Oliver Twist* isn't hard to understand, and neither is the imagery and symbolism. Evil people are described as dangerous animals or as typical stage villains. The weather is usually cold and rainy when bad things happen. This simplicity has helped to make *Oliver Twist* a very satisfying book to read.

FORM AND STRUCTURE

When you read *Oliver Twist*, you can read as quickly or as slowly as you want. If you are caught up in the action and can't wait to see what happens, you can read more. And when you finish the novel, you can go back and reread the parts you liked best. But when *Oliver Twist* was first published it appeared in monthly installments, each two or three chapters long, from February 1837 to March 1839.

Dickens knew that each installment in *Bentley's Miscellany* had to be exciting enough to leave the readers eager for the next one. He deliberately ended each section with unresolved situations or unanswered questions. One example is at the end of Chapter VIII, where Oliver falls into a deep sleep in Fagin's house. To find out what happened to the boy, readers had to buy the next month's magazine. To understand Dickens' technique, compare it to writing a television soap opera. Each segment is exciting in itself, at the same time it continues what happened the time before and makes you eager to find out what happens next.

Oliver Twist, like most other novels, has a begin-

SERIALIZATION OF *OLIVER TWIST* IN *BENTLEY'S MISCELLANY*

Chapter	Issue Date	Chapter	Issue Date
1,2	2/1837	28,29,30	4/1838
3,4	3/1837	31,32	5/1838
5,6	4/1837	33,34	6/1838
7,8	5/1837	35,36,37	7/1838
9,10,11	7/1837	38,39(part)	8/1838
12,13	8/1837	39(part),40,41	10/1838
14,15	9/1837	42,43	11/1838
16,17	11/1837	44,45,46	12/1838
18,19	12/1837	47,48,½49	1/1839
20,21,22	1/1838	½49,50,½51	2/1839
23,24,25	2/1838	½51	3/1839
26,27	3/1838	52,53	4/1839

Oliver Twist in its entirety was published in book form in November 1838.

ning, middle, and ending. The first eleven chapters cover Oliver's story from his birth to his rescue by Brownlow. The longer center section, Chapters XII through XXXIX, is complicated by the introduction of many new characters and events. Oliver is kidnapped, robberies are planned, and romances develop. Monks and Fagin plot to destroy Oliver. In the final chapters, from XL to LIII, all of the unanswered questions about Oliver's background are answered and he is finally rescued once and for all. The good characters are rewarded with the promise of future happiness, and the evil ones are punished.

While Oliver doesn't appear in every chapter,

the different elements of the novel are unified by his story. For example, Dickens describes Nancy's life and death very powerfully, but Nancy's primary importance in *Oliver Twist* is that she protects Oliver from Fagin and Monks. The same thing is true of Bumble. Dickens satirizes him and the whole system of treating the poor, but Bumble exists in the novel because of his relationship to Oliver.

In the very last chapter, Dickens lets you know that everything has worked out for the best, and that Oliver, the Maylies, and Mr. Brownlow can look forward to a happy life together.

The Story
CHAPTER I

Oliver Twist's story begins with his birth in a public workhouse in an unnamed English town. His unmarried young mother lives only long enough to kiss him lovingly on the forehead, dying before she can even give him a name or tell the workhouse her name. As an illegitimate workhouse orphan, Oliver seems doomed to a life of misery.

When the baby cries at his birth, the narrator ominously says that if the child had known what the future held, he would have cried louder.

NOTE: Workhouses were common institutions in nineteenth century England. They provided shelter for the unemployed poor. But to many people, including Dickens, they seemed places of punishment rather than charity. Pay attention to what Dickens has to say about this workhouse and the people who run it. The points he makes helped change terrible conditions by bringing them to public attention.

CHAPTER II

From the workhouse, Oliver is sent to the parish "baby farm." With little to eat, he becomes a small, pale child. He celebrates his ninth birthday locked in the coal cellar with two other boys. He is being punished for wanting more to eat. The parish decides the boy should earn his keep by picking oakum (a fiber used in caulking). Oliver is called back to the workhouse by Mr. Bumble, the parish beadle, whose job it is to oversee institutions run by the parish. Happy as he is to get away from the farm, Oliver feels lonely leaving the only home and friends he's ever had.

What impression does Mr. Bumble make on you? Some readers find his conversations and behavior amusing because he seems like such a buffoon. Others find the humor overshadowed by his cruel treatment of Oliver. As you read on, look for evidence to support your own reaction to him.

NOTE: One of Dickens' distinctive features as a novelist is the way he names his characters. Good humor or bitter satire are suggested by calling an incompetent meddler Bumble or a suspicious old man Grimwit. Twist, the name Oliver gets because Bumble names foundlings alphabetically, suggests the intricate web of his story and the twistings and turnings that await him before his story is unraveled.

Dickens attacks the workhouse through mockery and satire. The elaborate, formal language at the beginning of this chapter, which hides the simple fact that a baby needs food to live, is a good example of that approach. Dickens focuses on the inadequate diet of the youngsters in the parish's care to suggest a whole range of mistreatment, not only in this chapter but in the ones that follow. What impression do the fat parish authorities make in contrast?

The Board of Directors grills Oliver to be sure he knows how grateful he should be for all the generosity he's received. Oliver shows that he's learned an important lesson at the farm by never complaining about his treatment. He's willing to play along in order to avoid punishment. Based on his experience, how else would you expect Oliver to act? Does he seem passive here, or a shrewd survivor?

The Board of Directors seem absolutely indifferent to the child's suffering. Dickens exaggerates the situation he's satirizing, saying that the workhouse residents were fed only thin gruel with an onion twice a week and a half a roll on Sunday. But the anger Dickens feels about England's treatment of the poor is clear. This attack sets up one of the most famous scenes in the novel, Oliver's dramatic request for a second helping: "Please, sir, I want some more." Instead of being given more food, however, Oliver is thrown into solitary confinement. A notice is posted on the workhouse door offering £5 to anyone who will take Oliver Twist as an apprentice.

NOTE: Although *Oliver Twist* brought conditions in workhouses to wider public attention, reform was already underway by the mid-1830s. A new Poor Law had been passed in 1834 to improve conditions for orphans and paupers. But some of its provisions—the forced separation of families in workhouses, for instance—seemed very harsh. Further reform was needed.

CHAPTER III

After his bold request for more food, helpless Oliver is repeatedly beaten as a warning to others. To most readers, this seems an incredible punishment for being hungry. Dickens is exaggerating to make you sympathetic to this abused boy. Some readers feel he is exaggerating too much, thus reducing the power of his words.

Oliver's future darkens when Mr. Gamfield, a chimney sweep, applies to take the boy as an apprentice. Here, Dickens is attacking two things at once: the apprentice system and the horrible plight of chimney sweeps, who often were undernourished children valuable only because they could squeeze into narrow chimneys to clean them.

NOTE: The apprentice system This was a particular target for Dickens because of his own experience as an apprentice in a blacking factory. Apprenticeship was supposed to provide training for young men in a specific craft or trade. At the same time, it provided busy craftsmen with helpers in return for room, board, and training. Masters often abused their young apprentices, forcing them into miserable living and working conditions.

What kind of master is Gamfield likely to be? The first clue is found in the way he beats his donkey for no reason. Watch for other characters who abuse animals: it usually serves as a hint about their nature. Notice that a member of the workhouse board, seeing Gamfield beat the donkey, decides that Gamfield is the perfect master for Oliver. Between these two powers, what hope does Oliver have?

What saves Oliver from the dangerous job and brutal master? The half-blind magistrate who is about to sign Oliver's apprenticeship papers by accident happens to look at the little boy's terrified face and is moved to pity. Dickens is suggesting that Oliver's face is his most important asset; watch for it to save him again.

For the first time, something has worked in Oliver's favor. He is saved from Gamfield, but his problems are far from over. The sign advertising a boy "To Let" is posted again. Don't miss the irony in that choice of words. Dickens is emphasizing the board's inhumane attitude, which reduces Oliver to a piece of merchandise.

CHAPTER IV

Bumble sets out to find a way to ship Oliver off to sea, but he's saved the trouble by the local undertaker, Sowerberry, who's willing to take the boy on as a mourner. Mourners were hired to follow funeral processions to add to the solemn air of the occasion. This custom might seem odd to you, but Victorians took their funerals very seriously.

Sowerberry, like many of the characters in *Oliver Twist*, is a caricature. He represents a typical undertaker, sour and glum. Most readers think Dickens uses him, as he uses Bumble, not only to criticize bad individuals in the social system but also to show how people ignored the horrible conditions around them.

You might think Oliver is weak because he so willingly takes this assignment and tearfully promises to be a good boy. But Dickens explains his behavior by saying the boy has been so abused for so long that he has been reduced almost to "brutal stupidity and sullenness." While some readers think that Dickens sometimes lets emotional scenes run too long or uses exaggeration excessively, most of them are touched by Oliver's misery in this scene. Yet other readers feel that, if this were a more true-to-life novel, Oliver would become a hopeless delinquent by the time he was nine. Do you agree with that point of view?

Oliver yearns for kindness, but he doesn't get much from Mrs. Sowerberry. She resents any food she has to feed the boy, and the only place she is willing to let him sleep is with the coffins. Of course, his prospects have never been very bright, and you could say that he's as well off as he could hope to be.

CHAPTER V

As Oliver settles in among the coffins at Sowerberry's he begins to think death would bring the peace and calm he's never known. With morning comes more unhappiness. Oliver meets his new adversary, Noah Claypole, the bullying charity-boy employed by the Sowerberrys. Their dimwitted servant girl, Charlotte, is in love with him.

NOTE: The charity boy, unlike the workhouse orphan, was supported by his drunken father's tiny pension rather than by public funds. To Noah this distinction means that he is superior to Oliver, and he loses no time in demanding the privileges he feels due him. Dickens' biting satirical remarks on Claypole's self-importance are among the author's bitterest comments on human nature.

Dickens briefly describes Oliver's first outing as a mourner. The real point of the brief account, though, is to give another glimpse of the miserable conditions under which so many English people lived and died. Even the rats are hungry in the slum where a nameless young woman has starved to death. Yet Bumble and Sowerberry are indignant that her grieving family has the nerve to be proud rather than grateful to the parish.

CHAPTER VI

Sowerberry's business is good. There are many funerals in the months after Oliver is formally apprenticed, and he learns quickly. Noah Claypole grows jealous of Oliver's success.

Searching for a way to torment the boy, Noah sneeringly asks about Oliver's mother. For the first time, Oliver's anger is aroused. He cherishes the tiny scraps of information he has about her, and he won't allow Noah to belittle them. Attacking the larger boy in a fit of fury, Oliver knocks him to the ground. But Noah has allies while Oliver has none. Charlotte, Mrs. Sowerberry, and Noah beat the child until they are exhausted. Mrs. Sowerberry hypocritically claims that only good fortune kept Oliver from murdering them all. Even worse, she sends for Oliver's old enemy, Mr. Bumble, and locks the child in the cellar.

Noah made slurs on Oliver's mother only to taunt Oliver. Even today, people insult each other with comments about "your mother." But this style of insult takes on particular significance in *Oliver Twist*. You remember that Dickens begins the book with a brief but sympathetic description of the young mother. She is a mysterious figure, but watch for the hints Dickens continues to give you about Oliver's parentage—especially about his mother.

CHAPTER VII

Noah runs eagerly to find Bumble and to repeat the story of Oliver's attack on him. He groans and moans in such agony that he attracts the attention of the parish board's gentleman in the white waistcoat. When Bumble reports the lie that Oliver has tried to murder the Sowerberry family, the gentleman repeats once more his belief that Oliver was born to be hanged. Noah adds another lie—that Sowerberry wanted Oliver whipped.

Noah Claypole's phony tears and faked terror demonstrate the parish boy's worst side. He and Bumble are delighted at the thought of the punishment that awaits Oliver—a specific clue to their characters. Some readers believe, however, that Dickens overdoes this satirical humor. What do you think? Do you find it too heavyhanded? Or would you say the kinds of abuses deserve to be exposed by harsh ridicule?

Still locked in the cellar, Oliver isn't terrified of the beadle this time and even talks back. When

Sowerberry returns Oliver insists that nobody can insult his mother. This boldness only earns him two beatings, one from Sowerberry and the other from Bumble. Bumble explains Oliver's behavior by saying that Mrs. Sowerberry has given him too much to eat and he's developed too much spirit! The workhouse philosophy is to keep children hungry and thus passive, and Bumble insists it is a good philosophy. Is Dickens carrying his biting satire on hunger too far to be believable?

One thing is certain. When his mother's reputation is at stake, Oliver will not back down. It is only when he's banished to his gloomy coffin bed that he breaks into bitter tears. But the independence he's shown in defending his mother gives him new energy. He won't stay and be abused anymore. He decides to run away.

On his way out of town Oliver passes the workhouse farm where he'd spent nine miserable years. There he meets an old friend, a pitiful dying child named Dick, who kisses him goodbye and wishes God's blessing on him. Oliver is deeply touched, for these good wishes are the first he's ever had. Some readers feel that Little Dick's desire to die is too maudlin, and some even resent the scene's "tear-jerker" tone. On the other hand, it's hard to think of a sadder person than a child who knows he's dying from neglect and will be glad when he doesn't have to suffer any more.

NOTE: This chapter contains an example of an inconsistency in *Oliver Twist* that some readers find troublesome. At the end of the chapter Dick is weeding a garden. At the beginning of the next, it is winter, and only a few hours have passed. Such errors probably resulted from Dickens' writing the novel in serial chunks.

CHAPTER VIII

Oliver's life enters a new phase as he makes his way to London. Escape is on his mind, but so is the opportunity to make a new life. The walk (with only an extra shirt, two pair of stockings, a crust of bread, and a penny to his name) nearly does him in. Most of the people he meets are as mean as the ones he's left behind, but a kind old lady and a generous man working on the highway provide him with enough food and shelter to make his way to the little town of Barnet, at the northern edge of London.

NOTE: Dickens knew London intimately and used it as the setting for much of his fiction. His geographical descriptions of the city and the routes his characters follow through it are accurate to the most minute detail. Most of the neighborhoods he mentions still exist, although they've been altered over the years. You can find Barnet, Kensington, and Islington, for example, on a modern map, along with many of the street names Dickens used. St. John's Road, for example, is still a route into central London from the north.

The first person Oliver meets in London is often called one of Dickens' most brilliant creations. He is Jack Dawkins, better known as The Artful Dodger.

His flamboyant clothing is described at great length. So are his short, bow-legged body and his dirty, snub-nosed face. His speech is so full of slang, he almost seems to be speaking another language.

What's important to Oliver is that he's found a friend who feeds him and offers him lodging with a " 'spectable old gentleman." Oliver suspects that the Dodger is a bad risk, but he doesn't reject the offer of shelter. He hasn't much choice.

London's filthy streets, awful smells, and drunken residents worry Oliver as he and the Dodger make their way under night's cover to the slum known as Saffron Hill. Before he can decide to run away again, Oliver finds himself made right at home by another of Dickens' brilliant creations, the old Jew, Fagin. His villainous, repulsive face and his mat of red hair scare Oliver, but he offers food and a bed to Oliver. Warm, fed, and lulled by hot gin-and-water, Oliver falls into a deep sleep.

CHAPTER IX

Oliver wakes to find himself alone in the room with Fagin. Still drowsy, Oliver is quiet for a long time. Fagin, thinking himself unobserved, examines his secret horde of treasure. He muses on how capital punishment is a good thing because it keeps him safe from confederates who might tell on him.

For many readers Fagin is a supreme villain. They say that Dickens draws him as repulsive both physically and morally. For instance, when Fagin discovers that Oliver has been watching him, his first instinct is to grab a knife and kill the child. But his iron self-control is more powerful than his rage, so he calms himself and leaves the child alone. He easily persuades the innocent boy that the stolen treasures are all Fagin's own legal property. Looking at Fagin from a different perspective, however, you may feel that he provides a bit of kindness and security for the child. Some readers, on this evidence, refuse to believe that Fagin is all bad. As you read on, gather evidence for your own opinion.

Dickens took the name Fagin from a young man who had befriended him during his unhappy apprenticeship. Readers who have no sympathy for the fictional Fagin argue that Dickens must have felt that the real-life Fagin was tainted by his association with the cruel apprentice system. Otherwise, they say, Dickens would not have used a friend's name for such a man. Other readers say that naming the old man after a friend shows that Dickens didn't think the character completely evil.

NOTE: Fagin's Jewishness   You might wonder about Dickens' repeatedly calling Fagin a Jew. To modern ears it sounds anti-Semitic, and it is. In the nineteenth century the English were suspicious of all foreigners, and Jews were generally considered outsiders. Simply labeling Fagin a Jew would have moved many of Dickens' Victorian readers to judge him with suspicion. The notorious seller of stolen goods in London, Isaac (Ikey) Solomon, also a Jew, is considered Dickens' model for Fagin. One cliché that was associated with Jewish villains, including Ikey Solomon, was their excessive interest in money. Fagin is neatly tailored to fit that model.

Oliver's innocence is shown when he doesn't

understand either the kind of work the boys have been busy doing or the "game" of pocket-picking that Fagin has them play after breakfast. Fagin urges Oliver to model himself on The Artful Dodger.

Some readers are disturbed by Oliver's willingness to do what he's told. They think he is just too good to be true. Others argue, however, that Oliver is to be pitied, rather than criticized, for being innocent. This is the first of several episodes in which his innocence confronts the evil of the world. Keep track of them. They will help you make a final judgment about Oliver's character.

CHAPTER X

After intense practice, Fagin sends Oliver, his new recruit, to work. His more experienced boys, Charlie Bates and the Dodger, make Oliver nervous by picking on little boys and helping themselves to fruits and vegetables. Suddenly, the purpose of the game is clear. The Dodger and Charlie are picking the pocket of a distinguished gentleman who is looking at the books for sale or loan at a sidewalk bookstall.

Desperate to get away, Oliver runs off, only to be followed by shouts of "Stop, thief!" and a thundering crowd eager for blood. The two real culprits even join the pursuit! The chase ends when Oliver is knocked to the ground, but the gentleman who has been robbed, Mr. Brownlow, pities Oliver and goes with him to the police station.

CHAPTER XI

Oliver is taken to jail and locked in a dismal, smelly cell. Brownlow, troubled by Oliver's situation, has the strange feeling that he's seen the child somewhere before but he doesn't know where. He doesn't want to press charges, but he has no choice.

In the Metropolitan Police Office, the magistrate Fang (another name that pinpoints a character) is about to hear the case against Oliver. What happens here may seem outrageous to you, and Dickens intended it that way.

NOTE: The first English police force was established in 1829, just eight years before this part of *Oliver Twist* was written. Before that, the law had been very loosely administered. Many injustices still existed in 1837 and Dickens wanted them exposed. An actual magistrate, Laing, was the model for Fang; he was removed from office about six months after this episode appeared in print.

Fang is so rude and incompetent that Brownlow loses all respect for him. Even as he tells the story of the attempted robbery, Brownlow makes up his mind to protect the child. When Oliver is brought before the magistrate, he is so terrified he can't even say his name, and so sick that he faints. Despite this, Fang sentences the boy to three months at hard labor. Just in the nick of time the bookseller appears and testifies that he saw the other boys commit the crime. The case is thrown out of court. Without hesitation, Brownlow takes Oliver home with him.

After Oliver's brief and terrifying experience with crime, Dickens is ready to introduce a new phase in the boy's life. The opening of *Oliver Twist* introduced several mysteries. This chapter provides the first clues to solving them, but it also adds more mystery. For instance, why does Brownlow think he's seen Oliver's face before?

In what seems a lucky accident, Oliver's first adventure in the world of crime hooks him up with the one man in all London who will be able to solve the mysteries that surround him. Is this just a fortunate accident that might happen in anyone's life? Can you think of an example of a fortunate coincidence from your own experience?

CHAPTER XII

Oliver has another new home. Again, the first thing he does is sleep. Some readers have suggested Dickens is using sleep as a device to make transitions between Oliver's experiences, almost the way a moviemaker uses a dissolve to fade from one scene to another.

Oliver is unconscious for several days and awakens to a new and very different life. One of the most striking changes is that he, at last, finds a warm-hearted mother figure in Brownlow's housekeeper, Mrs. Bedwin. She wishes that Oliver's own mother could see how sweet he is. Oliver, meanwhile, is fascinated by a portrait of a lady hanging in his room. The child imagines that the figure in the portrait wants to speak to him. When Brownlow comes in to say hello, he is struck by the resemblance between the woman in that portrait and the child. As he exclaims at this, Oliver faints.

Just as the mystery of the relationship between the painting and the child seems about to be solved, Dickens totally shifts the scene, returning with Fagin's boys to their thieves' den. Dickens deliberately chooses to prolong the mystery, so that other episodes can follow. Up to this point it has been a straightforward tale of a boy's life, but from now on Dickens includes many scenes without Oliver. The novel describes many people that Oliver doesn't know, and these characters make the novel richer and more powerful. Dickens uses them to expand his social criticisms, and they are also the objects of his biting humor or of his pity. With them, Dickens can point out things that are wrong in Victorian society.

CHAPTER XIII

Bill Sikes, Fagin's partner in crime, arrives at the apartment. He's just in time to be drenched with the pot of beer Fagin has hurled at Charley Bates. The greeting does nothing to improve Sikes' temper, and his response is to kick his dog across the room. Remember Gamfield and his donkey? Dickens is once again using a man's abuse of animals to give a clue about his character.

The relationship between Sikes and Fagin is uneasy. Their careers are linked, but each knows too much about the other. Fagin acts afraid of the louder, more aggressive Sikes. Yet he makes it clear that Sikes is in danger because of what Fagin knows about him.

Fagin and Sikes discuss Oliver. They agree they must get him back before he gives the authorities any information about the gang. They send Nancy to find out what happened to Oliver at the magistrate's office. She discovers what you already know, that Oliver has been taken home by the gentleman the Dodger tried to rob. The gang has no option. Oliver must be kidnapped and the gang's headquarters moved.

Many readers think Nancy is fascinating even in

this brief introduction. They point to her independence and her bright spirit as she clowns about finding her "sweet little brother." Very briefly you get the sense of the raucous good humor that the gang shares. As you'll see, of all the characters in the novel, Nancy changes the most. Why does Dickens treat her differently from the other members of the gang? What is your evidence?

CHAPTER XIV

Back at Brownlow's, Oliver thrives. The eerie painting has been removed from his bedroom and is not mentioned again. New clothes replace his rags. At last the child is invited to visit his benefactor in his study.

Terrified that he will be sent away, Oliver begs Brownlow to let him stay. His old dread of loneliness still haunts him. Brownlow tells the boy he is welcome as long as he is worthy of trust. The older man explains that he's been disappointed in people in the past, but he senses that Oliver will not disappoint him. What does this seem to foreshadow?

Just as Oliver is about to tell the story of his life, they are interrupted by Mr. Grimwig, an old friend of Brownlow's, whose attitude toward people is nicely summed up by his name: He trusts no one.

NOTE: Dickens gives Grimwig a characteristic expression ("I'll eat my head") to help you remember who he is. Compare this to Fagin's "My dear" and Bumble's "porochial". In a novel with so many characters, this kind of "signature" helps you to remember who they are from one episode to the next.

Brownlow has some books which must be returned to the bookseller's. Oliver begs to be trusted with the errand and he sets out with Brownlow's blessing—and a warning to come straight home. Grimwig, not surprisingly, claims there's no chance the child will return. Do you think he's right? Are your reasons the same as his?

CHAPTER XV

Bill Sikes is in characteristic form as we meet him again in The Three Cripples, a seedy tavern. He starts this chapter by kicking his dog. But this time the beast objects and sinks his teeth into Sikes' boot. In a fury, the man raises his arm to strike the dog but is interrupted by Fagin's entrance. Sikes' black mood increases the tensions between the men, but you get a new insight into their dealings: Fagin controls the money and Sikes controls an effective information network. All that Sikes' blustering accomplishes is to make the secretive Fagin hate him.

During this confrontation Nancy, who is still on Oliver's trail, is in another room of the tavern. You learn that Sikes is attracted to her, and they leave together. Meanwhile Oliver is on his way to the bookseller's. Suddenly he is horrified to find himself firmly in Nancy's grasp. Their chance meeting is one of the theatrical details that make *Oliver Twist* so exciting to read.

Oliver's struggles and cries are in vain. A crowd gathers, but the people are willing to believe that the boy is delinquent and that his "sister" is right to take him home. In the clutches of Nancy and Sikes, Oliver is hustled away.

CHAPTER XVI

Crucial differences between Nancy and Sikes appear as they take Oliver back to Fagin. Sikes encourages his dog to growl at the boy and sneers at Nancy's sympathy for the prisoners who are to be hanged in the morning.

NOTE: The thought of death, especially death by hanging, haunts many members of Fagin's gang. Nancy imagines how the condemned men in the jail must feel on their last night, knowing what awaits them. Capital punishment was used frequently in England, and applied to many crimes including theft as well as murder. After 1839, only 8 crimes were still punishable by execution. But law-breakers knew that death by hanging was a very possible end to their careers. Here, Nancy's feelings foreshadow the many deaths to come.

Oliver, for all his own misery, senses a bond with Nancy when he feels her trembling as they walk toward Fagin's. You can see, too, that his reaction to Fagin is entirely different this time. Perhaps one reason is that he has Brownlow to compare to Fagin. The child begs to be allowed to leave, or at least to clear his honor by having the books and money returned to Brownlow. But the gang just laughs. Fagin in particular seems delighted that the boy will be thought a thief. Why do you think this pleases him? Watch for more of this attitude.

Oliver suddenly breaks away from them, and
Nancy shuts the door after him, insisting that Sikes
hold back the dog. In a moment of great tension,
Nancy screams that Bill will have to kill her first
before he harms the boy. (This is more foreshadowing.) After Oliver is dragged back, she grabs the
club Fagin is using to hit Oliver. Roused to fury
by their treatment of the boy, she threatens to betray them to the police. Fagin, Sikes, and Nancy
shout harsh truths at each other, and finally Sikes
wrestles the girl until she passes out.

What accounts for this radical change in Nancy?
Dickens never explains what makes her regret having brought Oliver back or what drives her into
frenzy. Some readers have suggested it is her ma-
ternal instinct. Others think there is a spark of human goodness which slum life hasn't yet put out.
Others point out that she's worked for Fagin for
twelve years; maybe she realizes what's in store
for the boy and wants to protect him from it. Can
you think of any other reasons? At any rate, her
protests are ignored. Oliver stays with the gang.

CHAPTER XVII

The narrator interrupts the progress of the story
to defend the dramatic value of digressions. This
sets the stage for going back to see what is happening in Oliver's birthplace. It also changes the
tone from melodrama back to satire, as you see
Mr. Bumble going about his parish business. He
meets Oliver's friend Little Dick, who appears to
be dying. Seeing this pathetic figure, how do you
feel about Oliver's fate?

Bumble goes to London on parish business. He
happens to read a newspaper advertisement offer-

ing a reward for information about Oliver Twist. Eager for the money, Bumble goes to Brownlow and smears the child's character. He's so persuasive that even Mrs. Bedwin's spirited defense cannot keep Brownlow from angrily writing the boy off as a little villain.

CHAPTER XVIII

Fagin devotes his energies to hooking Oliver into a life of crime. He threatens and pleads by turns. He puts the boy in solitary confinement until Oliver is grateful even to go out with the Dodger and Charley. When he judges the time ripe, Fagin creates such a congenial atmosphere the lonesome child is drawn, against his will, into the gang's society.

The most important element in this chapter is Dickens' skillful development of Fagin's character. You may even admire the psychological skill and single-minded determination of the old master criminal. But why do you think Nancy compares him to the devil?

CHAPTER XIX

Fagin's plan for ruining Oliver takes a giant step forward. He and Sikes are plotting a robbery, but have a hard time cooperating. Although Sikes won't confide any more details than he must, he does say he needs the assistance of a small boy. Oliver will be perfect, Fagin insists. Sikes needs a little persuading, but Nancy joins Fagin's side and urges the thief to use the boy. The one thing that Sikes and Fagin agree on is that Nancy is absolutely trustworthy. Do you think they are judging her correctly?

Do you wonder about Nancy's apparent change of heart? She doesn't protest Oliver's being used in the robbery. At this point, you learn that she is living with Sikes. Do you think that her love for him overrides her concern for Oliver? That's what Fagin thinks.

Dickens is very discreet about sexual matters. The text never mentions, for instance, that Nancy is a prostitute although Dickens identifies her that way in a preface to the novel. You don't get any physical details of her romance with Sikes, but that doesn't mean it isn't physical.

There's one more surprise too. When Fagin goes to tell Oliver he's to take part in a robbery, the boy is asleep. His innocent face touches the old man's heart. Is there really some humanity in Fagin? On the other hand, if Fagin were not touched by the child's innocence, what would that say about him?

NOTE: So far, no reason has been given for Fagin's determination to make a criminal out of Oliver. When Sikes asks him directly why he's so involved with one particular boy, Fagin is flustered, stammering an excuse, changing the subject. You'll discover later that there *is* a reason, which Dickens has not mentioned yet. Perhaps he is saving it for suspense, or perhaps he didn't plan out the whole story before he wrote it.

CHAPTER XX

Fagin seems to have trouble telling Oliver he is to go with Sikes, although he does nothing to change the plan. He's frustrated that Oliver isn't more interested, for it shows the boy's thoughts still aren't criminal. Yet before Fagin leaves for the evening he warns the child to beware of Sikes. His apparent compassion for Oliver makes Fagin a more complex character. What's more, Fagin seems very perceptive about Sikes and his capacity for violence. Why do you think he keeps on working with Sikes if he is so aware of his evil qualities?

Left alone to worry about the future, Oliver prays that he will not become a criminal and that he will be rescued from danger. Just as he finishes, Nancy enters his room. Dickens deliberately places these incidents together to emphasize Nancy's role as Oliver's defender. Oliver's innocent face affects Nancy deeply, but she explains to him that—in this instance—there is nothing she can do to protect him.

She warns Oliver that Sikes will kill him if he betrays the gang and shows him the bruises she's gotten for arguing with Sikes about Oliver's safety. But she makes no effort to interfere. She seems to sense how far she can go in defying Sikes.

CHAPTER XXI

Sikes and Oliver set out in the grey, cold, rainy morning.

NOTE: Dickens, like many novelists, uses weather as a clue to meaning. He chooses to make rain and fog suggest bad times, while sunshine represents happiness or justice. This connection between weather and feelings is powerful in *Oliver Twist* because it echoes many people's feelings. Notice that on nearly every evil occasion in the novel it is

dark or rainy, or both. No sun shines on the actions of Fagin and his gang, or on Oliver when he
is with them. In contrast, in other places later in
the story Dickens will use sunshine as a mark of
goodness. Then Oliver grows strong and healthy
and is happy. In literary terms, Dickens is using
weather as a metaphor.

The robbers head west through the streets of
London. In Kensington they get a ride that takes
them out of the city, and then resume their long
walk. Finally, at dinner time, they stop for a meal
in Hampton. They obtain a ride to Shepperton and
then walk until Oliver is exhausted. Late at night,
just as Oliver is convinced that Sikes has brought
him a great distance only to murder him, they find
themselves outside a deserted, dilapidated house.

CHAPTER XXII

Oliver is confused and silent while Sikes meets
up with the other gang members at the house and
they prepare for the crime. Armed and ready, the
gang sets out through the still-falling rain. Suddenly, as Oliver is hoisted over a wall surrounding
a private house, he realizes they are there to commit burglary. He begs to be allowed to run away,
but Sikes' answer is to point a gun at his head.
The others, Toby Crackit and Barney, stop Sikes,
although it isn't clear whether they want to save
Oliver or just get on with the robbery.

The boy is dropped into the house through an
opened window, chased by Sikes' threats. Determined to expose the crime no matter what the risk,
Oliver starts forward only to be frozen by Sikes'

command to come back. In the frenzy that follows, Oliver is shot, dragged back through the window, and carried swiftly away. As the clanging bells and shouting men fade into the distance, Oliver lapses into unconsciousness.

CHAPTER XXIII

The scene shifts to the workhouse where Oliver was born, and to Mr. Bumble's courtship of the workhouse matron, Mrs. Corney. The clumsy love scene between these two unromantic figures provides comic relief to a story that has become rather grim.

Dickens can be a master of comic dialogue, and the tone here never falters. Just as Bumble is about to propose, Mrs. Corney is summoned to the bedside of a dying woman who has a secret to tell. This gives Mr. Bumble an opportunity to calculate the value of her household property before he commits himself to marriage.

CHAPTER XXIV

The death watch at Old Sally's bedside is an unsettling episode. In spite of his sentimental comments about the peaceful faces of the dead, Dickens makes a harsh statement about human nature here, showing that greed and deception are as true of the poor as they are of their keepers. Can you explain how, when self-interest is involved, Old Sally and Mrs. Corney are very much alike?

At last some of the details surrounding Oliver's birth begin to emerge as Sally explains what happened the night Oliver was born. Oliver's mother had saved some gold to buy her baby "friends" if the infant survived, but Old Sally kept the gold, leaving Oliver poor and friendless. Where is the gold now? How much did the other old women lurking outside the door overhear? There are still many mysteries to clear up.

CHAPTER XXV

The scene shifts back to Fagin and his jolly gang of thieves. Waiting for the return of the robbers, they tease Tom Chitling unmercifully about his romantic attachment to Bet, a young friend of Nancy's. Just as things get out of hand, the doorbell rings. Toby Crackit (a good name for a burglar!) returns alone from the robbery attempt.

Fagin is beside himself, but Crackit won't talk until he's eaten. Toby's first comment drives Fagin into a frenzy, for he asks, quite seriously, "How's Bill?" Nobody knows. All Fagin has learned from the newspapers is that the job has failed. When he hears that Oliver was left lying in the ditch and Crackit doesn't know if the child is dead or alive, Fagin bursts from the room with a yell.

Don't you think it strange that Fagin is so concerned about the boy? So far Dickens has complicated the story of Oliver Twist without providing many answers. His main goal so far has been to arouse the reader's curiosity about the lonely orphan.

CHAPTER XXVI

Fagin makes his way to The Three Cripples. The landlord's man, Barney, hasn't returned from the robbery attempt, but Fagin seems much more interested in the whereabouts of a mysterious new character identified as Monks.

Leaving a message for Monks to call on him the

next day, Fagin talks casually with the landlord. You now learn for certain about something hinted at before—Fagin is an informer who sells information about his associates to the police. Does this knowledge lessen your opinion of Fagin or did you expect such activity of him?

Still disturbed about the missing child, Fagin makes his way to Sikes' apartment to confront Nancy. Trying to obtain information she might have, Fagin pretends to be concerned for Oliver. Though she's been drinking, she makes it clear that she wants the boy safely away from the gang. At the same time, she doesn't want anything bad to happen to Sikes. Fagin threatens Sikes' safety if anything happens to Oliver. For a moment, his iron self-control slips and he rages about losing a boy who is worth hundreds of pounds to him. Just as quickly he catches himself and forces himself to resume his usual smooth manner. He tries to discover if Nancy suspects anything. This deviousness is an important facet of Fagin's complex character.

Nancy is not stupid, and her behavior immediately changes, too. She insists that Sikes is on Fagin's side and stops defending Oliver. This time, though, her change of heart seems faked. She's a good enough actress to convince Fagin that she's too drunk to remember anything, and so he heads home.

NOTE: Drunkenness was a major problem for both men and women in London's slums during Dickens' lifetime. Cheap gin was a common drink. It was readily available and powerful enough to provide a quick high. Keep track, in particular, of

Nancy's use of alcohol. When she stops drinking, later on, she has a specific reason.

The mysterious Monks is waiting for Fagin when he gets home. They head for a deserted room and whisper together. At first you can't hear what they say. Monks then raises his voice angrily, insisting that Fagin made a mistake in sending Oliver on the robbery, rather than corrupting him gradually as he did with other boys. Fagin declares that approach wouldn't have worked because Oliver doesn't have a criminal nature.

From the conversation, you can figure out that Monks had spotted Oliver the day Brownlow was robbed. Monks had already been searching for this boy, so he convinced Fagin to get the boy back. You probably have begun to suspect that there is something very dangerous about Monks, but there's no way to tell, yet, what it is.

The conversation between the men ends when Monks is startled by the shadow he sees on the wall. Dickens is preparing you for the plot complications to follow.

CHAPTER XXVII

In an abrupt change of mood and scene, the story switches back to Bumble's courtship of Mrs. Corney. Nor is theirs the only romance in Oliver's hometown. The beadle bumbles in on Noah and Charlotte embracing in the Sowerberrys' parlor, and he's shocked at seeing the "lower orders" daring to kiss.

Some readers think this chapter's humor is heavy-handed. On the other hand, both romances are so odd that it's clear Dickens is making fun of the characters and their love lives. This makes perfect sense when you remember that he has poked fun at Bumble and Noah from the beginning. It is sometimes difficult, however, to see how these events fit into the story as a whole, but Dickens is using them to show the difference between real love and false love.

CHAPTER XXVIII

Five chapters have passed since Oliver was shot. Finally the story goes back to Sikes running from the scene of the crime, carrying the wounded child. On the verge of being caught, he lays down Oliver and speeds away after Crackit. The child's unconscious body lies undiscovered, however, because the servants of the house are terrified of really catching up with the thieves.

NOTE: Plot development Dickens was interested in making his plot dramatic. To do that, he didn't follow a strict chronological development, but built up the suspense by using digressions. Notice that Crackit, who is running away here, ate dinner at Fagin's in Chapter XXV. Sometimes you can't tell how much time is passing during the novel. This may have resulted from Dickens' method of writing one installment at a time. The only exception is at the dramatic conclusion, which he wrote all at once. Then, within one week, all the mysteries are solved, the guilty are punished and the innocent rewarded. Whether sticking to chronological order or not, Dickens always keeps you eager to find out what happens next.

As day comes, Oliver awakes. He's stiff with cold, drenched with rain, and racked with pain. Staggering toward the house, he faints on the doorstep. But the servants are so involved in reliving their chase of the robbers that they barely hear his knock. This scene increases the suspense and develops the comic characters of Giles and his sidekicks. Some readers who get frustrated with Dickens feel that delays show his limitations as a writer. Others insist the Dickens' ability to create suspense and keep readers involved in a story are some of the reasons his work is still so popular. If you read such Dickens' novels as *Great Expectations*, especially Pip's encounters with Magwitch, *A Tale of Two Cities*, or *Bleak House* you will find other examples of exciting stories using a similar technique.

As soon as they see Oliver, the men recognize him as one of the thieves. But the young mistress of the house insists the boy be put to bed. Delicately, she doesn't look at him just yet. This allows the story to take another complicating turn.

NOTE: Oliver is again in transition between Fagin's world and a new one. Once more, he sleeps deeply as he moves from one life to another.

CHAPTER XXIX

With Oliver comfortably in bed, and the doctor sent for, you meet the women of the house. Mrs. Maylie is stately and mature. The girl, Rose, a lovely seventeen-year old, is described glowingly.

NOTE: Women characters Dickens is often criticized today for the way he writes about women characters, especially the good women. Most modern readers find them too sweet and too dependent on other people to be believable. For example, they think that Rose Maylie, the heroine of *Oliver Twist*, is not as interesting as she could be because she does not seem to be realistic. In order to understand why Dickens wrote about Rose as he did, you have to understand that, in the mid-19th century, women were admired for being obedient to their husbands and parents, for being modest and discreet, and for not asserting themselves or their own ideas. That is exactly how Rose behaves.

As the women finish breakfast, the plump and talkative Dr. Losberne arrives to look after the patient. He is absolutely insistent that the women see the young thief. Dickens humorously shows Giles trying to postpone such an interview in order to bask a little longer in his false heroic glory. Unlike the attacks on Bumble or Noah, Dickens is only gently poking fun here. Dickens uses humor for different purposes. Sometimes the laughter is used to mock and ridicule. Sometimes it is just to make you laugh.

CHAPTER XXX

Dr. Losberne enjoys leading the women upstairs to see Oliver and he plays the scene for all it's worth. Dickens, however, seems to be carried away with the sad situation, indulging in sentimental observations about poor Oliver's unhappy life.

The women insist that any child who looks the way Oliver does can't be evil. Rose begs that they protect Oliver as she has been protected by Mrs. Maylie. This is the first clue that there is a mystery in Rose's background as well as Oliver's.

The doctor insists that they will quiz the boy and, if his story seems plausible, they'll keep him out of the clutches of the law. You may be bothered by Losberne's decision to flout justice by lying to the authorities. Or you may think about the representatives of the court system you've seen in the novel, and approve of Losberne's decision.

NOTE: Losberne strikes most readers as an endearing character despite his tendency to dramatize everything. One of the marks of Dickens' brilliance as a writer was his ability to create distinctive minor characters like Losberne.

Later that day, Oliver finally tells them his life story. Persuaded of Oliver's innocence, the doctor turns his energy to knocking down Giles' claim that the thief he shot was the child upstairs. But just as Giles is ready to change his story, the Bow Street Runners arrive. This split-second timing, melodramatic but effective, is another example of Dickens' genius in extending suspense.

NOTE: The Bow Street Runners were a semi-official group of police investigators who had been organized in mid-18th century. Their primary role was finding and arresting robbers. The bulk of their pay came from the recovery of the loot. The system was open to abuses, and by 1839 the Runners were replaced by professional police. Later in his life Dickens was a fan of the police, but that attitude is not evident in *Oliver Twist*.

CHAPTER XXXI

Blathers and Duff, the incompetent Runners, are fine products of Dickens' playful satiric wit. They search the scene of the crime, but all they find out is that the robbers weren't "yokels." They spend a lot of time interviewing Giles and his men, but they are confused by the butler's story. Finally, they are drawn by Losberne into a long description of their past adventures, which totally distracts them from the case at hand.

Losberne at last lets them see Oliver, claiming the boy was not wounded with Giles' gun. He doesn't tell the Runners that the gun they are inspecting isn't the one that was fired. Nor does Losberne let on that he removed the bullets from the gun. The Runners are convinced that Giles isn't very smart and isn't a very good shot either—exactly what Losberne wants them to think.

Losberne emerges in this chapter as a valuable friend of the women and of Oliver. Unlike Rose, he is shrewd enough to know that Oliver is doomed if arrested, and he manages to convince the gullible detectives that Oliver isn't their boy. Luckily, the next morning two men and a boy are arrested nearby, and so the investigation comes to a halt.

Saved from arrest, Oliver mends and thrives, exactly as he had when Brownlow rescued him in

Chapter XII. Are two lucky rescues too much to be believed? Or is Dickens saying that a person sometimes does get a second chance at happiness?

CHAPTER XXXII

The parallel with his earlier rescue is very clear to Oliver. As before, his gratitude knows no bounds. His delight at being rescued is a poignant comment on the dreadful experiences he's had. His only request is to try to get back in touch with Brownlow. What does this tell you about Oliver?

When Oliver is well enough to travel Dr. Losberne takes him to London to be reunited with Brownlow. But the trip is plagued by bad luck. In Chertsey, Oliver recognizes the house where the thieves had met before the robbery. Unwisely, Losberne goes to speak to the humpbacked man who lives there. Worse, he asks for Sikes by name and allows the man to catch a glimpse of Oliver. This encounter will no doubt lead to danger for the child.

Losberne admits that he has acted rashly because he was too eager to find evidence to back up Oliver's tale. Before he can dwell too much on that mistake, however, a new disappointment looms. Brownlow has apparently left for the West Indies. Rather than risk a further upset, Losberne refuses to go on to visit the bookseller. Oliver seems dismayed that he may never be able to clear himself in Brownlow's eyes.

The Maylies, sharing Oliver's dismay, close up their house and move to the country for the summer, taking the boy with them. The picture the narrator paints of the country and of Oliver's life there seems overly sentimental and too perfect to many readers. This happy situation seems to them unbelievable after what Oliver has been through. Other readers claim that the contrast is acceptable because *Oliver Twist* is almost a fantasy or a fairytale rather than a realistic novel.

CHAPTER XXXIII

Evil finds a way to enter even this perfect life. Rose falls desperately ill and Oliver, urgently consoling Mrs. Maylie and himself, insists that heaven would not let someone so beautiful and good die young.

Mrs. Maylie is too wise to believe him, but she struggles to keep calm. Once again Oliver is entrusted with an errand just as Brownlow entrusted him to run the errand to the bookseller. Oliver is asked to deliver an urgent letter to Dr. Losberne. Notice that *Oliver Twist* has many significant parallels in action and images like this one. At an inn on his way home, Oliver again meets a threat, when he runs into an unnamed man who greets him with the terrifying shout: "Death!" Cursing, the man moves aggressively toward Oliver only to fall on the ground writhing and foaming in a fit.

Oliver rushes home to new trouble, as Rose grows worse. The beautiful summer day seems to be at odds with the little boy's misery. Seeking solace, Oliver stumbles into the local cemetery where a child's funeral is in progress. After that omen, he can't believe that Rose's youth and beauty will protect her from death. Suddenly, however, the crisis passes. The sunshine was a clue that things would be all right, but Oliver hadn't believed it. Dickens reassures the reader that miracles do happen. Rose will live.

NOTE: Rose Maylie's near-fatal illness recalls, in every way except its happy conclusion, the unexpected illness and death of Dickens' beloved sister-in-law Mary Hogarth in May, 1837. When Mary's funeral was over, Dickens was so emotionally upset that he could barely work. He even missed an installment of *Oliver Twist*. His feeling of love for Mary and great loss at her death is echoed in this novel, and also in *The Old Curiosity Shop, David Copperfield, Little Dorrit*, and many other of Dickens' books.

Because he is so overjoyed at Rose's recovery, Oliver hasn't had the time to worry about his encounter with the strange man. But you may. The suspense grows more complicated.

CHAPTER XXXIV

Oliver is so happy Rose is better that he can barely control his glee. So is another unknown gentleman who arrives with Giles in tow, desperate for news of the girl. He is Mrs. Maylie's son Henry (called Harry).

Henry claims he loves Rose, but that doesn't seem to impress his mother. In fact, she tries to discourage her son's affection and you get the impression that she doesn't think he's sincere enough. But you do learn what the cloud hanging over Rose is: there is some shame about her birth—probably she was illegitimate.

NOTE: It is important to realize how powerful the consequences of sexual immorality were for

Victorian women. Bumble's disapproving attitude was cause for satire early in the novel, but now when rational Mrs. Maylie talks about morality, you see how important it was to Victorians. Pay careful attention to what Rose knows and to what you learn about her actual family.

As time goes by and Rose recovers, the dream-like summer seems to protect them all from danger. Oliver studies as diligently as he had begun to do at Brownlow's. Even in this paradise, however, the devil is a threat. Oliver wakes from a nightmare about Fagin to find the old man's evil face peering in the window. And with him is the nameless, violent stranger from the inn!

When Oliver recognizes them they disappear. As soon as he recovers from his terror, Oliver screams for help. Dickens has been careful to point out the clues (like the man in Chertsey in Chapter XXXII) which would have led Fagin to the boy, so this visit seems entirely plausible. We know how determined the old thief is to get Oliver back.

CHAPTER XXXV

The next day, the Maylie household can find no evidence of Fagin's visit. Once again, Oliver's experience can't be proved. Why do you think Dickens included this scene?

Soon Oliver's scare is forgotten. The romance between Harry and Rose takes center stage. At last Harry proposes, but you discover that true love isn't always easy—or happy either.

You've already had a hint of the blot on Rose's reputation, which she believes will hurt Harry's career. Sobbing, Rose insists he deserves a more suitable wife than she could be. But she also admits that she loves him and would marry him if he were not destined for fame and fortune.

Are you convinced that Rose really believes what she says, and that Harry believes it too? Notice that Dickens seems to accept that Rose's apparent illegitimacy could destroy her husband's career. Dickens doesn't even seem to be protesting that situation, as he does the effects of the Poor Laws or the criminal justice system. A Victorian's view of Rose's situation would probably have been quite different than a modern reader's view.

CHAPTER XXXVI

This brief chapter provides a bit of information and more suspense. Harry is running for Parliament with the help of his powerful uncle. When he takes off in a great hurry after Rose refuses him, she concludes, unhappily, that he's not upset about her refusal. But you learn that he's made Oliver promise to write and let him know everything that happens to Rose. Can you figure out what Harry is going to do?

NOTE: Parliament is Great Britain's legislative assembly and governing body. It is divided into two branches, the House of Commons and the House of Lords. Representatives are chosen for the House of Commons in elections that must be held at least once every five years. The political party that wins the largest number of seats usually chooses the prime minister, the head of Great Brit-

ain's government. Today, the House of Lords has
little influence, but in the 1830s it had considerable
importance. Members of the House of Lords are
not elected, but are members because of titles they
hold.

CHAPTER XXXVII

Bumble's unhappy marriage is a complete contrast to Harry and Rose's blighted romantic dreams.
Gloomy and depressed, Bumble misses the beadle's hat he gave up when he married Mrs. Corney
and became master of the workhouse. We now see
him as a hen-pecked wreck of a man who yearns
for his lost freedom.

NOTE: Many readers think that if you compare
this scene shift to the one at the beginning of
Chapter XVII, you can see how much smoother
and confident Dickens has grown as a novelist.
There Dickens seems to think the digression is
strained and awkward, because he felt he had to
apologize and explain what he was doing. Here
the shift seems to provide natural comic relief to
Rose's unhappy love story.

In a pub, Bumble meets an odd stranger who
has been looking for him. You aren't told his name,
but you may guess from his haunted look and dark
scowl that it is Monks.

The visitor is willing to pay for information about
the woman who nursed Oliver Twist's mother. Ever
greedy, Bumble says he knows someone who can

provide the information and he agrees to meet the man again.

CHAPTER XXXVIII

An ominous storm brews the next night as the Bumbles go to meet Monks in a crumbling building at the river's edge. Doesn't the scene remind you of meetings between Fagin and his gang?

Tough Mrs. Bumble insists that Monks pay £25 for her information, even before he's heard it. He produces the money and she tells him that Old Sally had stolen the gold from Oliver's mother's corpse and pawned it. After Sally died, Mrs. Bumble took Sally's pawn ticket and redeemed a gold locket. She shows it to Monks. Inside are two strands of hair and a wedding ring engraved "Agnes." The date engraved inside is within a year before Oliver's birth.

NOTE: Some careful readers have pointed out an inconsistency here. In Chapter I, as Oliver's mother dies, Dickens gives no hint of this theft and Sally is not mentioned by name. In Chapter XXIV, Sally tells Mrs. Bumble that she had stolen gold that the dying girl could have used to buy food and shelter. It is hard to tell if Dickens added these details to make his story more exciting, or if he had forgotten what he wrote months before.

Monks admits that the ring and locket were what he hoped to find. He opens a trap door in the floor beneath their feet and throws the packet into the rushing water below, destroying evidence of Oliver's identity. Shocked into silence, the Bumbles make their way out into the night.

You probably can't figure out the significance of this episode to Oliver's future. You know other things about Monks' involvement, but Dickens doesn't want you to grasp the whole picture yet. Notice Dickens' use of suspense as he spins out the interview between Monks and the Bumbles. If this were a movie, you'd be on the edge of your seat.

CHAPTER XXXIX

In a miserable rented room, Bill Sikes has fallen on hard times. While he's been sick, Nancy has stuck with him and nursed him. Yet now that he finally feels strong enough to get up, he hits her and then curses her for whining. Only when she faints does he become concerned. Why does Nancy put up with his abuse?

NOTE: Your attention is focused on Nancy in the next few chapters. Trace the conflict she feels between loyalty to Sikes and love for Oliver. Think about how she has changed since the unsuccessful robbery attempt.

Fagin arrives with food and drink, but Sikes wants money. He insists that Nancy go home with Fagin to get it. While Nancy is at Fagin's, Monks is also there. She reacts violently to the sound of his voice, tearing off her bonnet and shawl. She pretends not to take much notice of him, but she stares at him intently when he isn't looking.

As soon as Fagin and Monks leave the room she sneaks along behind them and eavesdrops on their conversation. Now you know whose "shadow" Monks saw in Chapter XXVI.

Once more, Dickens makes you wait in suspense to find out what Monks and Fagin discuss. All you know is that the conversation upsets Nancy so much that she runs wildly through the streets until at last she heads home in despair.

Nancy manages to hide her feelings from Sikes. Ironically, just now Bill says to her he's positive she'd never betray him. But she betrays him a little, right now. She laces his liquor with laudanum (a common 19th-century drug) to be sure he'll sleep. Then, kissing him, she goes out on a secret errand. Who is it that she rushes through the night to see? Rose Maylie!

But the mission nearly fails. The staff at Rose's hotel wants to protect ladylike Rose from meeting a disreputable street girl. Again, Victorian morality is strict against sexual offenders. Nancy responds differently than Rose would to the insults. First she shouts, then she begs, until she gets her message to Rose and is asked in. How can you explain her determination to succeed on this errand?

CHAPTER XL

The narrator briefly interrupts the flow of the story to comment on Nancy's shame and her pitiful pride. Why does he draw attention to her low status?

NOTE: Dickens' insights into human behavior are an important part of his great reputation as a writer.

One of the major themes of *Oliver Twist* is the life-long consequences of how the young are treated. Nancy and Rose are the clearest examples of the difference a childhood can make. This interview provides a chance to see them together, to observe the differences between them, and to feel sorry for Nancy's misfortune. Since Dickens time, many psychiatrists, psychologists, and sociologists have studied the effect childhood has on people's behavior. Sigmund Freud's work, for instance, shows how very perceptive Dickens was about the relationship of early experiences and how people behave as adults.

The story Nancy has to tell Rose is shocking. She has twice overheard the man who calls himself Monks talking with Fagin about Oliver. She has discovered Monks knows the boy's parentage and has destroyed the evidence that proves it. Now Monks will get the inheritance that Oliver should have had.

Nancy describes Fagin's failed plan to make the boy a thief and warns of Monks' urgent wish to destroy him. Rose is surprised to hear that Oliver is Monks' brother. But she has a greater shock in store.

With her warning given, Nancy is anxious to head home. Rose urges her to stay, promising to protect her, but Nancy firmly refuses. Rose means to be kind, but many readers feel that she is condescending. How do you respond to the way Nancy is treated here?

NOTE: Women criminals For many people in Victorian England, including Dickens' readers, it seemed hard to believe that a woman could be a criminal or a prostitute willingly. They often explained women's crimes or immoral behavior by saying that the women had been misled by evil men. One response to women who broke the law was to punish them severely, so that other women would avoid crime. Another response was to reform them by teaching them to be domestic servants. This attitude reflects the idea that if women were dependent on good people, they would be good too. Dickens was more liberal than most of his countrymen in his approach to helping these women. He knew that few of them would want to—or be able to—make such a total transformation. Of course, many women like Nancy lived their entire lives in a criminal environment.

Nancy openly says she needs to return to her lover, though she is careful not to mention Sikes' name. Nancy doesn't seem to realize that if Fagin is caught, Sikes is bound to be. She still seems innocent, despite all the evil she's seen. What does this tell you about her? And how do you react when she says that she would go back even if she knew Sikes was going to kill her?

Recognizing that Nancy won't change her mind, Rose asks what she should do now with this information. Nancy urges Rose to find a man to help her. (Nineteenth-century women were not expected to act for themselves.) The women agree to set up a way to meet again and share information.

As she leaves, Nancy tries to explain once more that the only thing left in her ruined life is her devotion to her man. To many readers, the morbid sentimentality of the parting is almost too much to bear. They want Nancy to have a chance at happiness.

CHAPTER XLI

The next day Oliver spots Mr. Brownlow in the street. Rose seizes on Brownlow's reappearance, seeing him as the perfect confidante. After a warm reunion with Oliver, Brownlow listens to Rose's story. He immediately assumes control of the situation.

How is it that the Maylies happened to be in London just now? How did Nancy know where to find Rose? And what miracle makes Oliver spot Mr. Brownlow in the street the very next day? Without those coincidences the plot would have stalled, so Dickens makes them happen.

Taking Dr. Losberne and Mrs. Maylie into their confidence, Rose and Brownlow decide to solve the mystery of Oliver's parentage and get him his inheritance.

Brownlow doesn't contact the police because he wants information, not criminal prosecutions. Furthermore, he is willing to shield Nancy, hoping she will agree to help them find Monks. Do you think he's justified in this decision? Why?

Oliver's protectors agree to include Mr. Grimwig and Henry Maylie in their investigation. But Brownlow adds another twist: he suspects that his unexplained visit to the West Indies bears on the case. He begs them not to question him, though, until he's ready to say how.

CHAPTER XLII

Dickens breaks the suspense created in the last chapter as he comically describes Charlotte and

Noah Claypole making their way to London. They've robbed the Sowerberrys and are setting out to make a new life for themselves. Noah is careful, though, to let Charlotte carry the stolen property. Then he can't be blamed if they are caught.

By a lucky accident, the first place they stop when they get to the city is Fagin's haunt, the Three Cripples. Given the number of taverns in London, you might feel this is hard to believe. On the other hand, Dickens has located this pub on the route Noah probably would have taken. And, in the final analysis, you could argue it probably isn't as important how Noah ends up with Fagin as it is that he does.

Barney, who works at the Cripples and is a member of Fagin's gang, pegs the pair as potentially useful to Fagin. When the old man comes in, Barney sets him up to eavesdrop on Noah's conversation. Soon, Fagin joins the couple at their dinner table and recruits them into his service. Dickens seems to enjoy describing the master crook, conning these unsympathetic clods.

CHAPTER XLIII

Fagin introduces Noah to the life of crime. Candidly, Fagin explains his philosophy of life. The most important idea in the world, he insists, is that everyone must look out for himself. Noah is an eager pupil. Most readers agree that Dickens brilliantly depicts Fagin here as a total degenerate. Others argue, though, that Fagin is a portrait of a typical businessman, even if he happens to be working in crime rather than in a legitimate business. What is your opinion of him here?

Charley Bates arrives to tell Fagin the story of the Artful Dodger's arrest and his performance in court. Fagin and Charley humorously imagine the Dodger's cocky response to his treatment. Noah—who now calls himself Morris Bolter—is sent to the court to watch the Dodger's trial, which is just as lively and spirited as his friends imagined. The Dodger swaggeringly defies the court and attacks the character of its officers. Some readers suggest that what the Dodger is doing is carrying on with Oliver's request for "some more." Do these two scenes seem related to you? In what ways?

NOTE: In the courtroom scene, the Dodger makes a mockery of justice. This description, like the one of Fang's hearing in Chapter XI, conveys Dickens' criticisms of the criminal justice system. Keep these details in mind when you consider why Brownlow sidesteps the police and courts.

CHAPTER XLIV

Nancy behaves now like a different person. She admits to herself that Fagin and Sikes have trusted her and that her conversation with Rose is a betrayal of them. To soothe her emotions, she tells herself she's done nothing to harm Sikes. Is she fooling herself or does she really believe he won't be caught? Do you think she has betrayed him? What arguments would you use to support your opinion?

On Sunday Nancy tries to keep her rendezvous with Rose but she arouses the suspicion of Sikes and Fagin when she tries to slip out of the apartment. They lock the door, and not even her screams persuade them to let her go. Sikes is furious, but he tries to believe she's acting strange because she's sick. Fagin thinks perhaps she is fed up with Bill. He's determined to find out what's going on. If Nancy has a new lover, Fagin thinks he might be recruited to his gang. But even more important, he hopes Nancy could be persuaded to poison Sikes to protect herself and her new lover from the bully's rage. How wonderful it would be to get rid of the man he hates, secure a new ally, and increase his influence over Nancy all in one fell swoop!

Ever practical, Fagin decides to get the evidence he needs to blackmail Nancy by having her followed for a while. What does his new scheme add to your perception of Fagin?

CHAPTER XLV

Noah Claypole is doing well as a mugger, but Fagin has new plans for him. When Noah discovers it means spying on a colleague, he's delighted. On the next Sunday night when Nancy sets out again, Noah is trailing her.

CHAPTER XLVI

The dark London night is a fitting setting for Fagin's evil plan, but it also helps to hide Nancy as she goes to meet Rose. Nancy is restless, but fortunately she doesn't have to wait long for Rose and Mr. Brownlow to show up on London Bridge. The devious Noah Claypole hides within earshot. Though she has no way of knowing he's spying nearby, Nancy is haunted by visions of death. What does this foreshadowing tell you?

NOTE: Attitudes toward criminals During the nineteenth century there was a significant shift in the public attitudes toward criminals. The old idea was that people chose to commit crime. That was later modified to acknowledge the influence of environment on human behavior. In *Oliver Twist*, Dickens shows examples of both theories. Fagin and Sikes are evil by choice, while Nancy is unable to escape from the influence of the slums.

Nancy explains how she'd given her lover laudanum, a drug made from opium, so that she could get away the first time, and why she'd missed their appointment the week before. Brownlow insists he will not reveal to the police anything Nancy tells him, as long as Monks tells him what he wants to know about Oliver. Whatever happens, he promises to get Nancy's consent before exposing Fagin. This is another instance in which Brownlow is willing to work outside the law.

Nancy describes Monks to them. As he hears the description, Brownlow joins in, describing a distinctive burn mark on Monk's neck. Brownlow seems upset; Nancy is amazed. One more piece of the puzzle is about to be uncovered, but it's still not enough to give you the total picture.

Once more Brownlow and Rose beg Nancy to accept their help, but she insists she cannot. She must go home. She views this decision with dread, but she doesn't flinch from what the future holds for her. When she tells Rose she will probably drown herself, she is simply describing the fate of many hopeless women of her time.

How do you react to this scene? Dickens clearly

wants you to care about Nancy and to worry about her fate. What details has he used to evoke that response in you?

CHAPTER XLVII

Dickens begins this chapter by talking about Fagin in nonhuman terms that suggest he is frightening or dangerous. Worlds like "lair," "phantom," and "fangs" describe the old man's house and his physical appearance. This isn't the first use of animal imagery to suggest Fagin is scary or dangerous in *Oliver Twist*. Fagin has been described before as a reptile and a predator. Many writers have used animal imagery to express a sense of evil. Is Dickens suggesting that Fagin is about to act like an animal? Or is his need for revenge a strictly human evil?

After Noah delivers his report, Fagin is furious with Nancy. When Sikes enters, carrying the loot from his night's work, Fagin unnerves him by staring fixedly, speechless and twitching with emotion. The old man tells Sikes his story, masterfully rousing Sikes to a pitch of rage at the hint that the gang has been betrayed. Deliberately increasing the tension, Fagin wakes Claypole to make him tell Sikes about Nancy.

Fagin draws out every detail of Nancy's conversation from Noah. But he doesn't mention her desire to protect everyone but Monks or the fact that she chose to return to Sikes rather than be rescued. Sikes rushes from the room in a frenzy of rage. Fagin stops the robber briefly on the stairs to ask a loaded question: "You won't be—too—violent, Bill?" Sikes and he exchange meaningful looks, and Fagin modifies his comment: "I mean not too violent for safety."

With a terrifying singleness of purpose and a savage passion Sikes heads home. Remember the violent crimes he's committed before, and remember how many times Fagin has informed on other accomplices who weren't useful any more. Is Nancy's case any different for Sikes? for Fagin? Dickens asks you to consider whether violence against people who love and trust you is worse than random violence.

Nancy is pleased when Sikes returns. This makes his bloody murder of her even more chilling. Nancy begs for her life. She clutches desperately at him, trying to make him understand that she chose to stay with him. Brownlow will rescue them both, she promises, and they can find new lives. But her pleas are useless. Sikes is beyond reason.

Sikes knows he'll be discovered if he fires his gun, so instead he smashes her face with it. Dying, the girl tries to pray. She holds up the white handkerchief Rose has given her. But Sikes strikes her down with his club.

CHAPTER XLVIII

The narrator insists that of all the dreadful things ever done in London, Nancy's murder was the worst, the foulest, and the most cruel. Should you take that comment at face value, or do you think Dickens is using overstatement to emphasize Nancy's tragic death?

Narrators are not simply representatives of the novelists who create them. You, the reader, should be able to mark the difference between the narrator's ideas and the author's. At the same time, when an author feels strongly about something you can often detect the author's voice in the narrator's comments. That interlocking of narrator and author occurs frequently in *Oliver Twist* and in other Dickens novels.

The description of the morning after Nancy's murder is graphic and dreadful. The apartment is a total mess. Even the dog's feet are bloody. The darkness that shrouded London's underworld until now is suddenly replaced by brilliant sunlight. Many readers think the reason Dickens uses sunlight here is to suggest that such dreadful evil will be uncovered and exposed. Sikes tries to draw the curtain to block out the light from the grisly scene in the room. But he can't do it, any more than he will be able to prevent what happens to him.

Sikes can't control his own emotions. Inside the room he is careful never to turn his back on the corpse with its haunting eyes. Though he leaves home to wander through the streets of London, he unwillingly returns to the same place. When night comes, he makes his way to a pub in Hatfield, only to meet a traveling salesman wanting to demonstrate a miracle drug by removing a blood stain from Sikes' hat! Sikes runs wildly away from the pub, but when he passes the post office and he overhears the mailcoach guards gossiping about the murder, he can't help but listen, torturing himself.

Sikes is convinced Nancy's corpse is following him. Running, dodging, turning, he tries to escape from it, but to no avail. Her eyes follow him everywhere.

The narrator's voice interrupts with Dickens' message that a murderer cannot escape judgment. If no one punishes him, he punishes himself. Do you agree with Dickens' viewpoint?

Two strange incidents reveal the twists of Sikes'

character in this chapter. His nightmare journey to escape from Nancy's haunting eyes is interrupted by a major fire at a local firm. He joins fearlessly in the struggle to extinguish the fire. Miraculously, nothing seems to harm him, and he briefly blocks out the memory of his crime. But when morning comes, the news of the murder is on everyone's tongue and he sets out once more—this time back to London. Then, suddenly convinced that his dog will give away his presence in London, Sikes decides to drown it in a nearby pond. The dog manages to run away, however, and Sikes travels on alone.

CHAPTER XLIX

Brownlow wastes no time rounding up Monks and bringing him back to his house to question him. He tells Monks he has two options—either cooperate or be turned over to the police. This frightens Monks, and he agrees to talk with him. One thing is immediately clear. Monks knows who Brownlow is, just as before Brownlow seemed to know who he was. You learn now that Brownlow was Monks' dead father's oldest friend. Identifying Monks by his real name—Edward Leeford— Brownlow tells him that he knows about his brother Oliver. Monks tries to deny everything, but Brownlow tells what he knows: that his friend Leeford had been forced into the early and miserably unhappy marriage which produced Monks. Later, after the marriage fell apart, he had fallen in love with a young woman who loved him in return and whom he hoped to marry. Brownlow had learned all this many years before from the elder Leeford. But soon after the unhappy man died suddenly, leaving no will. His estate passed entirely to his legal wife and legitimate child.

Leeford, however, had left a portrait of his fiancée in Brownlow's care, and Brownlow gathered that the girl was pregnant. After his friend's death Brownlow went looking for her, but she had disappeared.

Monks is relieved to hear that the fiancée could not be traced. That means there is no evidence about his brother's identity. But Brownlow floors him again by saying "a stronger hand than chance" had delivered Oliver Twist into his keeping. Monks nearly falls off his chair! He knows all about how Oliver found a patron and how the boy was kidnapped and returned to Fagin. Nobody, however, had told him the patron was Brownlow!

NOTE: Effective coincidences This is a coincidence that most readers feel works because it is exactly the kind of thing that really does happen in life. Pay attention to the details that unravel Oliver's true identity in this chapter and in Chapter LI. Are they believable? Decide for yourself, as the plot winds to an end, whether it takes too many coincidences to bring about the happy ending.

Brownlow did not at first know that the ragamuffin he rescued was his friend's illegitimate son. But Oliver's strange attraction to the woman's portrait in Brownlow's guest room, and the striking resemblance between the boy and the painting, triggered a suspicion in Brownlow's mind. After the boy was kidnapped, Brownlow made inquiries and discovered who Oliver really was.

Next, Brownlow tells what he learned from Nancy, that Leeford *had* left a will which his wife destroyed, and that Monks had recognized Oliver in the street because he was struck by the child's resemblance to his father.

Brownlow continues to present his evidence against Monks. He knows that Monks destroyed the proofs of the boy's identity. He reminds Monks that Nancy died because she tried to protect Oliver. Monks finally relents and says he will confess all. But Brownlow wants more. He wants Oliver's inheritance restored.

At that crucial moment, Dr. Losberne interrupts the interview to announce that Sikes' dog has been spotted and the murderer is about to be arrested. Don't miss this little twist of fate. Ironically, Sikes' intuition was right—his dog did give him away.

CHAPTER L

The horrible environment of the London slums has been Fagin's home all along, but the apartment on Jacobs Island where his gang is hiding almost defies the imagination. Dickens goes to great lengths to recreate the squalor that he, as a newspaper reporter, knew existed, but which most of his readers had never seen.

NOTE: Many readers of *Oliver Twist* suggest Dickens is attacking the whole society for allowing such conditions to exist. They argue that while characters like the Maylies and Brownlow are generous as individuals, they are part of a culture which, to its shame, lets the Bumbles run its workhouses and the Fangs judge its criminals. Such a society ignores the existence of slums but is disgusted at its products.

The thieves gathered in this retreat reveal that Fagin has been arrested and that Claypole has turned state's evidence. Noah, who was encouraged by Fagin to spy on Nancy, is now willing to spill everything he knows about Fagin, too. When late at night, Sikes—a ghost of his former self—raps at the door, his former friends don't want to let him in. Charley Bates can't control his hatred. Calling him a monster, he jumps at Sikes. Sikes is ready to break the boy's neck but he's stopped by Crackit and the sound of a mob outside.

NOTE: This angry mob seeking to take justice into its own hands isn't the only such mob in *Oliver Twist*. Remember the mob that caught Oliver when he was accused of being a thief? Dickens had seen lots of violent mobs in London, including those at public executions. He found them very disturbing. So, even here, when its quarry is the murderer Sikes, Dickens makes the mob so terrifying and bloodthirsty that it is not much better than the villain being pursued.

Determined to escape, Sikes grabs a rope to let himself down into the smelly, stagnant ditch behind the building. Tying one end to the chimney, he makes a noose to fasten around his body and lower himself over the wall. Then, just at the instant that he slips the loop over his head, he looks around in horror and shrieks "The eyes again!"

Sikes plunges through space, the noose tightening around his neck until, with a tremendous jolt, the rope runs its length. Sikes is executed. The lifeless hand of the killer still clutches a knife.

Readers agree that this is an effective, thrilling scene, but many think the final detail is pathetic or ridiculous: howling dismally, Sikes' dog hurls itself at his master's shoulders, only to miss and bash its brains out in the ditch. In spite of his master's abuse, has the dog remained loyal to the end? If it has, then you can agree that it wants to share Sikes' fate. But you might also think that the dog's death is included to break the tension created by Sikes' hanging. If so, you might wonder if Dickens wants you to feel sorry for the dog or to think it is foolish for following such a cruel master to its death.

How do you feel about Sikes' violent death? Is it fitting punishment for Nancy's murder or is it just more senseless violence? Think about how you feel about the execution of murderers today. Does any crime justify a death sentence?

CHAPTER LI

Two days later (time is counted very carefully in these last chapters), Oliver finds himself, in the company of all those dear to him, on the road back to his birthplace. He's eager to find his old friend Dick and share his good fortune. But an air of unresolved mystery still hangs over the journey.

When they reach their destination, some answers are waiting. Oliver finally meets his half-brother, whom he recognizes as the stranger who threatened him one day at the inn. Although Monks can barely contain his hatred for his little brother, he finally tells his whole sordid tale.

When Mr. Leeford died, Monks' mother destroyed a letter he had left for Agnes, Oliver's mother, begging Agnes' forgiveness for not telling her why they couldn't get married right away. Monks' mother also destroyed the will naming Oliver as his father's heir.

In that will, their father stipulated that his illegitimate son would inherit everything, but only if he grew to adulthood without committing any crime.

NOTE: Many readers believe the plot is weakened by making Oliver's inheritance ride on such a strained condition, but Dickens uses this detail to introduce a serious idea. Leeford insists that goodness could not be measured by conventional morality, and that his "child of sin" should not automatically be branded an outcast. This refutes Victorian ideas of propriety, but it also suggests the elitist idea that true nobility is inherited, and has nothing to do with middle-class morals.

Robbing her rival's child of money wasn't enough for Monks' mother, though. She spread rumors about Agnes' family, driving the girl's father to despair and early death. She also begged her son to hunt down his brother and destroy him.

This chapter ties up all the loose ends. Mr. Grimwig exposes the Bumbles' involvement in Monks' scheme. Defending himself, the blustering former beadle delivers his finest line: "The law is a ass!" he exclaims, when told that the law assumes that husbands control their wives' actions. But his greed has finally cost him the public's trust and the Bumbles lose their job.

And what of Rose? Why has Mr. Brownlow dropped so many hints that she'll need to be strong? The last twist of Monks' story reveals that she is Agnes Fleming's younger sister, and therefore Oliver's aunt! Monks' evil mother had spread the rumor that Rose Fleming was illegitimate in order to further hurt the family. But Rose had been spared the misery of a orphan's life by Mrs. Maylie, who had witnessed her suffering and rescued her as a small child.

Rose's emotional reunion with Oliver is followed by a happy ending to her romance. Henry Maylie, who had helped Brownlow find Monks, once more begs her to marry him. She still insists that she is tarnished by her sister's shame and cannot change her mind. Henry is ready for her though: he's not a politician any more but a clergyman, so there is no need to worry now about hurting his career. Discreetly, Dickens omits the lovers' happy reunion.

But there's one last sad note to this emotional evening. Oliver discovers his friend Dick is dead.

CHAPTER LII

Oliver and his friends deserve the happiness they've found, but what will become of Fagin? In this moral tale, the good characters are rewarded. What happens to the evil ones?

Fagin is tried and convicted on a Friday and sentenced to hang on the following Monday. The crowded courtroom roars its delighted approval of the sentence, and even his fellow prisoners revile him. Does this treatment make you feel sorry for him? Or do you feel he deserves what happens to him?

NOTE: The English trial system dealt efficiently with the accused. If court was in session, a criminal case came before it immediately. The longest delay was three months. Final disposition of a case took a few days and there was no way to appeal a case to a higher court in the 19th century. Reprieves were sometimes granted, but Fagin didn't get one.

Confined to his cell, Fagin is obsessed with the thought of hanging. His conscience tortures him, his body is racked with fever, and his mind wanders. The narrator suggests that the sight of such misery would unsettle anyone's sleep. Yet Brownlow and Oliver come to visit. Brownlow tells Oliver that, since he saw Fagin while he was powerful and successful, he ought to see him now. Does that argument persuade you, or do you think there are some things that children should be kept from seeing? In any case, the boy is so upset that it takes him several hours to recover enough strength to walk away.

Oliver has escaped the gallows that hung over his life. Fagin will not. A mob has already begun to gather to watch him die.

CHAPTER LIII

The mysteries are all solved. The forces of evil are destroyed. Monks, because he was born a gentleman, is allowed to escape from England. But

Dickens is careful to add that Monks' corrupt nature led him to death in an American prison. Charley Bates, in contrast, was so shocked by Sikes' death that he reformed and went to work on a farm.

Finally, just so there's no question about the happy ending, Dickens describes in glowing terms the idyllic life Oliver, his family, and his friends enjoy in the English countryside. Dickens can't resist a wonderful final touch—the Bumbles have become paupers confined to the workhouse where they had abused their power. There is justice after all!

A STEP BEYOND

Tests and Answers
TESTS

Test 1

1. Noah Claypole torments Oliver about _____
   A. his funny way of talking
   B. his mother's reputation
   C. having to follow funeral processions

2. Bumble believes that the Sowerberrys' big- _____
   gest mistake with Oliver was
   A. making him sleep in the coffin room
   B. letting him go to school
   C. giving him too much to eat

3. The "game" Fagin plays with his boys is to _____
   make them better
   A. pickpockets   B. liars
   C. courtroom witnesses

4. The biggest advantage Fagin has over Sikes _____
   is his
   A. blackmail information
   B. connections with the police
   C. brains

5. Mr. Losberne's attitude toward the police _____
   is best expressed by which statement?
   A. A stitch in time saves nine
   B. The end justifies the means
   C. Nothing ventured, nothing gained

6. Rose rejects Henry's proposal because _____

A. she doesn't think he loves her
B. his mother is opposed to the marriage
C. she thinks she'd hurt his career

7. Nancy finds out about the plot against Oliver _____
   by
   A. eavesdropping
   B. opening a letter from Monks by
      mistake
   C. tricking Fagin into telling her

8. Mr. Brownlow knew Monks because _____
   A. Monks is his illegitimate son
   B. Brownlow had defended him in court
   C. Brownlow was Monks' father's friend

9. Dickens suggests that Monks' evil charac- _____
   ter is a result of
   A. his parents' unhappy marriage
   B. a blow to the head
   C. the slums where he grew up

10. Oliver's best piece of luck is _____
    A. inheriting a lot of money
    B. finding friends and family who love
       him
    C. meeting The Artful Dodger

11. Compare the evil Fagin intends for Oliver with what
    Brownlow tries to provide.

12. How does environment help to explain what hap-
    pens to the characters in *Oliver Twist*?

13. Compare the characters of Bumble and Fagin in their
    relationship to Oliver.

14. Discuss the comic elements in *Oliver Twist*.

15. Analyze the ways in which Dickens creates suspense in *Oliver Twist*.

Test 2

1. The parish sells Oliver as an apprentice because   _____
   A. he is a troublemaker
   B. of a provision in his mother's will
   C. he has potential to succeed

2. The major satire of the early chapters of   _____
   Oliver Twist is directed against
   A. religious institutions
   B. educational programs
   C. public servants like Bumble

3. Dickens uses rain as a symbol of   _____
   A. regeneration and nurturing
   B. evil events and environments
   C. the uncontrollable power of nature

4. Gamfield and Sikes are similar because they   _____
   both
   A. work with Fagin
   B. are able to brutalize Oliver
   C. mistreat their animals

5. Rose Maylie urges her aunt to care for Oliver   _____
   because she
   A. is grateful for her own good fortune
   B. thinks her nephew deserves good
      fortune
   C. knows that's what Brownlow wants

6. Noah Claypole finds his proper place in life   _____
   by becoming a
   A. private investigator   B. master thief
   C. police informer

7. Brownlow suspects from the beginning that   _____
   Oliver is a gentleman because he
   A. has excellent table manners
   B. resembles the portrait Leeford left
      behind
   C. studies hard and learns so quickly

8. Sikes meets his death by   _____
   A. being executed in Newgate
   B. being assaulted by an angry mob
   C. accidentally hanging himself

9. Which of the following statements reflects   _____
   one of the novel's themes?
   A. one bad apple spoils the bunch
   B. opportunity only knocks once
   C. as the twig is bent, so grows the tree

10. The beginning of the end for Fagin's gang   _____
    is
    A. Nancy's death
    B. The Artful Dodger's trial hearing
    C. kidnapping Oliver

11. Identify two things in society that Dickens attacks
    in *Oliver Twist* and explain why they are examples
    of social injustice.

12. Discuss the role coincidence plays in *Oliver Twist*.
    Contrast the ways it is effective and the ways it isn't.

13. In what ways áre Rose Maylie and Nancy different
    and how are they alike?

14. Describe the role of parents and parenting in *Oliver
    Twist*.

15. How does Dickens use imagery and symbolism in
    Oliver Twist?

ANSWERS

Test 1

1. B   2. C   3. A   4. C   5. B   6. C
7. A   8. C   9. A   10. B

11. To answer this question, think about the different ways Oliver is treated. He is fed and clothed by Fagin and the Brownlows, but that's where the similarity ends. Fagin thinks of Oliver as a valuable resource, who can be trained to be a pickpocket and help support the gang. When Monks offers Fagin money to corrupt the boy, he becomes even more valuable to the old man. Finally, Fagin knows Oliver can always be betrayed to the police. Find specific comments in the text that support these ideas. Brownlow's concern is for Oliver, not for what he can get from him. He offers education, too, but from books. He promises that as long as Oliver deserves his trust, the boy will be welcome. Discuss Brownlow's purpose in conspiring with others to change Oliver's future.

12. Since Dickens himself suggested that Nancy and Rose offered the best contrast of the effect of different environments, you could use them as examples.

As a starter, point out the ways in which the girls are similar (orphans, young, kind to Oliver, seeking love). Then discuss the surrogate parent who raised each of them (Fagin, Mrs. Maylie). Describe the physical surroundings in which they live. Finally, turn your attention to their sexual experiences and the role that immorality plays in their lives. The best scenes to use to illustrate your points are the ones where they are with their lovers, and those when they meet each other.

Another way to approach the question would be to analyze Oliver's response to different environments, and compare him to more hardened members of Fagin's gang, like the Dodger or Charley Bates.

13. Both Bumble and Fagin try to teach Oliver. To compare the two, describe how each tries to instruct the child, and why each fails. Finally, you might suggest some other ways that these two men resemble each other even though they seem quite different. Both are greedy, both are willing to betray their friends, and both come to bad ends.

14. Since there are many kinds of comedy, begin by defining them. Dickens uses puns, name-gags, descriptions, coincidences, and inflated language, as well as satire and irony to make his readers laugh. One effective approach is to compare the humor that is intended to amuse (like naming Bumble for his bumbling actions) and humor that is intended to criticize or expose (like the descriptions of the magistrate Fang). Since the novel was written in 1837–38, you might comment, too, on what kinds of humor continue to appeal to a modern audience and what kinds seem dated.

15. Most often the suspense is strongest at the ends of chapters, as some new clue or unexplained incident is introduced. Discuss how publishing in serial installments contributed to Dickens' plot structure, and relate this to other works you know that do the same thing. Then discuss the way the suspense builds throughout the book to the resolution in the last chapters. Evaluate how effective the suspense is by discussing what events in the story take you by surprise.

Test 2
1. A   **2.** C   **3.** B   **4.** C   **5.** A   **6.** C
7. B   **8.** C   **9.** C   **10.** A

11. Because Dickens is attacking both individuals and institutions, you have the option of focusing on either. Once you decide, though, be consistent. If you use individuals, talk about the problem of workhouses by discussing Bumble and the problems of the courts by describing Fang. Be sure to show how specific examples stand for broader criticisms. For example, Gamfield is one terrible apprentice master, but he also represents all such masters. Agnes Fleming and Nancy between them represent a wide variety of "fallen women." Fagin and Sikes show different sides of the criminal problem. An effective way to organize an answer which involves an entire book, as this one does, is to discuss things in the order in which they appear. Try to discuss examples from throughout the whole book.

12. First, explain what you mean by coincidence and distinguish it from chance, good luck, or divine providence. If you have a strong opinion about Dickens' use of coincidence, state it. Then, in the body of the answer, choose several examples of coincidence, being sure to include both effective and ineffective ones. For example, discuss Nancy showing up where Monks and Fagin are talking, Bumble reading Brownlow's newspaper ad, or Rose and Oliver unsuspectedly being related to each other. Explain how your examples support your opinion. If you don't have a strong opinion, explain why some examples of coincidence work and others don't. First discuss those that work and then those that don't by using examples from the novel. In your conclusion, explain the effect that coincidence has on the novel.

13. Because the most obvious things about Rose and Nancy are the differences between them, you can summarize those details briefly and then develop the ways they are alike. You should consider superficial things like their age as well as more important details, like the fact that both are orphans who have been brought up by guardians and both are involved in love affairs that seem doomed. Since their most important resemblance

is the love they feel for Oliver, develop that similarity most completely.

14. Parents, and surrogate parents, have an enormous influence on the young people in this novel, yet there isn't one intact family in the story. The two married couples—the Sowerberrys and the Bumbles—have no children. Nancy, Rose, Oliver, and presumably the boys in Fagin's gang are orphans. Monks and Harry Maylie are brought up by their mothers. In organizing your answer, one approach is to compare the parents or surrogate parents that do a good job (for instance, Mrs. Maylie or Brownlow) with those who don't (for instance, Mrs. Leeford, Bumble, Fagin). Be sure to point out what makes them different. In the case of surrogate parents, comment on what motivates them to take on the responsibility for a child.

15. Begin your answer by defining imagery and symbolism. Imagery is often explained as the use of visual pictures to suggest ideas or feelings. Symbolism usually means the use of one object or entity to mean something else. In this novel you can identify images, like the dark and dirty apartment where Fagin lives, or the animals to whom he is compared. Those details emphasize for the reader the environment in which the gang lives. Others are associated with happiness (the Maylie cottage), fear (the eyes that haunt Sikes), or greed (the plump trustees of the workhouse). Examples of symbolism include the fog and rain of London which signify evil, the sunshine which suggests goodness, and the repeated motif of hanging which suggests the choking effects of a life of crime. To complete the answer, discuss how Dickens uses these literary techniques to make the novel richer and more powerful.

Term Paper Ideas and other Topics for Writing

Characters

1. Bumble and Fagin both prey on children. Discuss how that characteristic helps condemn them in your eyes.

2. Oliver has several surrogate parents in this novel. Discuss the role of a parent in bringing up a child and show how Oliver's experience illustrates what good and bad parents are like.

3. How is Fagin like other memorable villains? It might be particularly interesting to compare him to demonic characters like Satan (in John Milton's *Paradise Lost*), Edmund (in William Shakespeare's *King Lear*), Iago (in Shakespeare's *Othello*), or Chillingworth (in Nathaniel Hawthorne's *The Scarlet Letter*).

4. Discuss the character of Sikes as a typical criminal. You might compare his reaction to Nancy's murder to his response to other crimes. Or you might compare him to Roskolnikov (in *Crime and Punishment*).

Themes

1. How do Dickens' various "love stories" show the many sides of human experience?

2. Identify and discuss the elements in London's underworld which Dickens suggests make that environment unhealthy.

3. What does Dickens mean by alienation? Compare its effects on several different characters. It's probably wise to include someone who triumphs over it (like Oliver) with someone who is defeated (like Nancy).

4. Is justice really achieved? Compare what happens to Bumble, Fagin, Sikes, and Monks.

5. Compare the theme of the good and evil brothers. You can refer to other examples from literature like Cain and Abel in the Bible or Edgar and Edmund *(King Lear)*.

Literary Topics

1. Discuss Dickens' varieties of satire. What is effective and what isn't? What are his purposes in using satire?

2. How does Dickens depend on coincidence to move his plot forward? Discuss the strengths and weaknesses of this technique.

3. Discuss Dickens' technique of using names to denote character. You might consider why this is more true of the minor characters than the major ones.

4. Discuss the use of digression to extend the mystery. Is it effective or not?

Outside Sources

1. Read the descriptions of Dickens' early life and compare his experiences with Oliver's.

2. Compare *Oliver Twist* with Dickens' *David Copperfield* in terms of a young boy's exposure to brutal, unfeeling people.

3. Discuss anti-Semitism in 19th-century England as it relates to *Oliver Twist*.

Further Reading
CRITICAL WORKS

Bayley, John. "Oliver Twist: 'Things As They Really Are,' " in *Dickens and the Twentieth Century* edited by John Gross and Gabriel Pearson. Toronto: University of Toronto Press, 1962.

Carey, John. *Here Comes Dickens: The Imagination of a Novelist.* New York: Schocken Books, 1974.

Cockshut, A. O. J. *The Imagination of Charles Dickens.* New York: New York University Press, 1962.

Colby, Robert A. "Oliver Twist: The Fortunate Foundling," in *Charles Dickens,* edited by Wendell Stacy Johnson. Englewood Cliffs: Prentice-Hall, 1982.

Collins, Philip. *Dickens and Crime.* Bloomington, Indiana: Indiana University Press, 1968.

Daleski, H. M. *Dickens and the Art of Analogy.* New York: Schocken Books, 1970.

Dupee, F. W., ed. *The Selected Letters of Charles Dickens.* New York: Farrar, Straus & Cudahy, 1960.

Fielding, K. J. *Charles Dickens: A Critical Introduction.* Boston: Houghton Mifflin, 1964.

Forster, John. *The Life of Charles Dickens.* 3 vols. Philadelphia: J.B. Lippincott, 1874.

Gissing, George R. *Critical Studies of the Works of Charles Dickens.* New York: Greenberg, 1924.

Greene, Graham. "The Young Dickens," in *The Dickens Critics,* edited by George H. Ford and Lauriat Lane, Jr. Ithaca: Cornell University Press, 1961.

Hardy, Barbara. "Dickens and the Passions," *Dickens Centennial Essays* edited by Ada Nisbet and Blake Nevius. Berkeley: University of California Press, 1971.

Hobsbaum, Philip. *A Reader's Guide to Charles Dickens.* New York: Farrar, Straus, & Giroux, 1973.

Johnson, Edgar. *Charles Dickens, His Tragedy and Triumph.* 2 vols. New York: Simon & Schuster, 1977.

Kettle, Arnold. "Dickens: *Oliver Twist,*" reprinted in *The Dickens Critics* edited by George H. Ford and Lauriat Lane. Ithaca: Cornell University Press, 1961.

Marcus, Steven. *Dickens: From Pickwick to Dombey.* New York: Basic Books, 1965.

Miller, J. Hillis. *Charles Dickens: The World of His Novels.* Cambridge, Mass: Harvard University Press, 1958.

Orwell, George. "Charles Dickens," in *Dickens, Dali, and Others: Studies in Popular Culture.* New York: Reynal & Hitchcock, 1946.

Pearson, Hesketh. *Dickens: His Character, Comedy, and Career.* New York: Harper and Brothers, 1949.

Tillotson, Kathleen. "Oliver Twist," in *Essays & Studies,* New Series, XII (1959), 87–105.

Wheeler, Burton M. "The Text and Plan of *Oliver Twist,*" in *Dickens Studies Annual.* Volume 12. New York: AMS Press, Inc., 1983.

AUTHOR'S SELECTED MAJOR WORKS

1836	*Sketches By Boz*
1836–1837	*The Pickwick Papers*
1838–1839	*Nicholas Nickleby*
1840–1841	*The Old Curiosity Shop*
1841	*Barnaby Rudge*
1843	*A Christmas Carol*
1843–1844	*Martin Chuzzlewit*
1846–1848	*Dombey and Son*
1849–1850	*David Copperfield*
1852–1853	*Bleak House*
1854	*Hard Times*
1855–1857	*Little Dorrit*
1859	*A Tale of Two Cities*
1860–1861	*Great Expectations*
1864–1867	*Our Mutual Friend*
1870	*The Mystery of Edwin Drood* (unfinished)

Glossary

Beadle Minor parish official who policed behavior in the churches and other local institutions.

Blunt Money, especially cash.

Bow Street Runners   Semiprofessional detectives who were the forerunners of the English police. Founded in the mid-eighteenth century by Henry Fielding, they were disbanded in 1839.

Covey   Man, often a young man. Usually used in slang or informal street language.

Cribbage   Card game for two to four players, in which the score is kept by inserting small pegs into holes arranged in rows on a small board.

Daub   Mistress or whore, in the sense that the women's reputation is marred or smeared.

Fence   Receiver of stolen property who arranges for it to be sold or sells it himself.

Fogle-hunter   Thief whose specialty is stealing silk handkerchiefs.

Hackney coach   Two-wheeled vehicle drawn by one horse; the common taxi of the 1830s.

Hoptalmy   Word referring to a disease of the eye, perhaps opthalmia.

Jack Ketch   Hangman or executioner.

Lagging   Term of imprisonment.

Laudanum   Opium derivative, commonly used as a pain reliever. It is addictive after long use.

Mute   Silent mourner in a funeral procession. The silence was supposedly caused by grief, but the mute was hired for the job.

Newgate Calendar   Publication containing accounts of prisoners in the infamous Newgate prison. It was a frequent source for fiction.

Oakum   Loose hemp or jute fiber, sometimes treated with tar. Used for caulking seams in wooden boats.

Peach   To inform on.

Plate   Term for money, originally referring to a piece of silver such as flat-ware or serving pieces.

Ridicules   Slang version of *reticules*, lady's purses.

Shilling   Unit of English currency. In Dickens' time, 20 shillings made a pound, and 12 pence (pennies) made a shilling.

Swag Property, booty. When Fagin and Sikes discuss "bringing off the swag" they mean committing a robbery.

Transportation Penalty for convicted felons who were not hanged. It meant the prisoner was sent abroad, often to Australia, and usually for life.

Victuals Pronounced "vittles," food fit for human consumption.

Whist Card game played by two teams of two players.

The Critics

On Content

Oliver Twist was a bold departure from the genial tone of *Pickwick Papers.* Instead of safely echoing the humour and hilarity that had set all England roaring with affectionate laughter, Dickens embarked on a scathing denunciation of the new Poor Law and moved on to a lurid and sombre portrayal of London's criminal slums. The comedy had a bite he had seldom previously attempted even in painting the Fleet or describing Dodson or Fogg. Bumble, the workhouse beadle, is comic, but the laughter has an acid quality and Bumble is slowly subjected to a kind of vindictive ferocity.

His fusion of bravery and instinct justified itself. Masses of readers hated Bumble and laughed at him with an angry laughter; they loathed Fagin and shuddered at Sikes. The pathos and horror of Dickens were as triumphant as his humor had been.
—Edgar Johnson, *Charles Dickens,*
His Tragedy and Triumph, 1977

On the Plot

The plot of *Oliver Twist* is very complicated and very unsatisfactory. It is a conventional plot about a wronged woman, an illegitimate baby, a destroyed will, a death-bed secret, a locket thrown into the river, a wicked elder brother and the restoration to the hero of name and property. That it should depend on a number of extraordinary coincidences (the only two robberies in which Oliver is called upon to participate are perpetrated, fortuitously, on his father's best friend and his mother's sister's guardian!) is the least of its shortcomings. Literal probability is not an essential quality of an adequate plot. Nor is it a damning criticism that Dickens should have used his plot for the purposes of serial-publication, i.e., to provide a climax at the end of each instalment and the necessary twists and manoeuvres which popular serialization invited. (It is not a fault in a dramatist that he should provide a climax to each act of his play, and the serial instalment is no more or less artificial a convention than the act of a play.) What we may legitimately object to in the plot of *Oliver Twist* is the very substance of that plot in its relation to the essential pattern of the novel.

—Arnold Kettle, *An Introduction to the Novel*, 1951

On Structure

At the heart of the book is the contrast between two worlds: and it is this which gives it some of its strange power. The criminal underworld seems dangerous. By the end a whole mob has to rouse itself against Sikes with passion and fury. Fagin is described as having fangs like a rat, and crawling forth at night like a 'loathsome reptile . . . in search of some rich offal for a meal.' Dickens certainly meant that Sikes and Fagin were menacing and corrupt, that they were infesting and undermining society, and that the upper classes were right to have the feeling of insecurity.

—K. J. Fielding, *Charles Dickens, A Critical Introduction*, 1964

On Oliver

It is important to remember that we do not identify with Oliver in the ordinary sense of the word. He is not, strictly speaking, a hero. Rather he is the embodiment of goodness; a means of setting society

in perspective. He acts as emblem rather than character, and the distancing effect is achieved by an
irony that, in the earlier chapters, hardly ever lets
up.

—Philip Hobsbaum, *A Reader's
Guide to Charles Dickens*, 1973

It is notable that Dickens makes no serious effort to
present Oliver with any psychological realism: his
reactions are not, for the most part, the reactions of
any child of nine or ten years old; he is not surprised
by what would surprise a child and his moral attitudes are those of an adult. And yet something of
the quality of precocious suffering, of childish terror, is somehow achieved. . . . Because he is *all*
workhouse orphans the lack of a convincing indi-
vidual psychology does not matter; it is Oliver's situation rather than himself that moves us and the
situation is presented with all of Dickens's dramatic
symbolic power.

—Arnold Kettle, *An Introduction to
the Novel*, 1951.

On Nancy and Rose

At the end of the novel we discover that Rose, like
Nancy, may be said to have opened her eyes on the
streets, in the sense that she was left helpless and
abandoned in childhood; and we may infer that she
would have been likely to go the way of Nancy if
she had not been provided with a home, first by
the "poor cottagers" who took her in, and then by
Mrs. Maylie. Rose and Nancy, in other words, are
counterparts—"Two Sister-Women" is the descriptive headline (added in the 1867 edition) to the
chapter which describes their first meeting—and the
fact that Rose is respectable and Nancy a fallen
woman is in no way to be attributed to the operation
of the principle of Good. Nancy is a victim not of
her nature but of social circumstance—she, indeed,
rather than Oliver, carries the victim theme of the
novel; Rose, on the other hand, is saved if not by
luck, then by the grace of God—and home. Both of
the girls, moreover, are dramatic counterparts of
Oliver. Rose is an Oliver who is saved from the

workhouse; Nancy is an Oliver whose goodness does
not save her from the streets.

—H. M. Daleski, *Dickens and the
Art of Analogy,* 1970

On Nancy and Sikes

Few would now wish to attack or defend Nancy on
moral grounds, her unreality as a literary creation
removing her from the area of discussion: it is an
index of changing taste and outlook that she could,
at that time, arouse such denunciations, or, indeed,
high praise from many critics who had misgivings
about the moral tendency, or the literary quality, of
other aspects of the book. It is not Nancy, but Bill
Sikes, who still excites our interest, and raises critical and moral problems. . . .

—Philip Collins, *Dickens and
Crime,* 1968

On Humor and Bumble

Dickens' refusal to allocate any emotions to his comic
figures is well illustrated by Bumble. Though Bumble is meant to be a hypocrite, it is his great innocence which strikes us, for he has no inside to himself for him to be untrue to. When we see Bumble
counting Mrs. Corney's teaspoons, weighing her
sugar tongs, inspecting her milk jug, and ascertain-
ing to a nicety the exact condition of her furniture,
before deciding to propose marriage to her, we are
not filled with disgust but with trepidation foresee-
ing, as he cannot, what is in store for him when he
wins Mrs. Corney's hand. It is not as if Bumble *could*
ever feel love, or even lust, for anyone, so why
should we blame him for regarding marriage as a
financial venture?

—John Carey, *Here Comes Dickens,
The Imagination of a Novelist,* 1974

Printed in the United Kingdom
by Lightning Source UK Ltd.
120456UK00001BA/10